"Sue Havala . . . is providing a true service to all of us who want to integrate wholesome foods into our daily lives."

—Mollie Katzen, author of
Moosewood Cookbook and
Vegetable Heaven and host of
Mollie Katzen's Cooking Show

"This terrific little book provides a right-on commonsense guide for anyone trying to find the jewels at the heart of the 'natural food' maze. Reliable information sits right where you need it alongside mouthwatering suggestions for simple, quick ways to make the very best use of the most nutritious and economical selections on every aisle of the natural foods store."

—Laurel Robertson, author of
Laurel's Kitchen Recipes
and *The New Laurel's Kitchen*

Most Berkley Books are available at special quantity discounts for bulk
purchases for sales promotions, premiums, fund-raising, or educational use.
Special books, or book excerpts, can also be created to fit specific needs.

For details, write: Special Markets, The Berkley Publishing Group, 375
Hudson Street, New York, New York 10014.

The Natural Kitchen

The Beginner's Guide to
Buying and Using Natural
Foods and Products

Suzanne Havala, M.S., R.D., F.A.D.A.

BERKLEY BOOKS, NEW YORK

NOTE: Research about human nutrition is constantly evolving. While the author has made every effort to include the most accurate and up-to-date information in this book, there can be no guarantee that what we know about this complex subject won't change with time. Please keep in mind that this book is not intended for the purpose of self-diagnosis or self-treatment. The reader should consult his or her physician regarding all health concerns before undertaking any major dietary changes.

THE NATURAL KITCHEN

A Berkley Book / published by arrangement with
the author

PRINTING HISTORY
Berkley edition / January 2000

The Penguin Putnam Inc. World Wide Web site address is
http://www.penguinputnam.com

ISBN: 0-425-17307-0

BERKLEY®
Berkley Books are published by The Berkley Publishing Group,
a division of Penguin Putnam Inc., 375 Hudson Street,
New York, New York 10014.
BERKLEY and the "B" design
are trademarks belonging to Penguin Putnam Inc.

PRINTED IN THE UNITED STATES OF AMERICA

10 9 8 7 6 5 4 3 2 1

In loving memory of
feline companions
Lois and Cindy

"A loaf of bread," the Walrus said,
"is what we chiefly need:
Pepper and vinegar besides
Are very good indeed."

—LEWIS CARROLL,
   Through the Looking Glass

CONTENTS

ACKNOWLEDGMENTS

It is my pleasure to acknowledge those who helped bring this book to life, beginning with my editors at The Berkley Publishing Group, Jessica Faust and Lisa Considine. Jessica and I shared a vision of a beginner's guide to natural foods that was simple and spare, taking the newcomer by the hand on an overview tour of the store, showing him or her a smattering of great products to try for starters, explaining some of the jargon, and providing the resources for anyone with an itch to learn more. Lisa helped refine that vision and with an expert eye guided the project through to completion.

My thanks to the rest of the team behind the scenes at Berkley who also worked on this book.

My heartfelt thanks to my friends and colleagues at the Vegetarian Resource Group and in Vegetarian Nutrition, a dietetic practice group within the American Dietetic Association, as well as others, who continue to share their expertise, ideas, and support, and who inspire and motivate me with their enthusiasm and sincere desire to help educate the public about good nutrition and to advocate for improvements in health and nutrition policies.

I am ever grateful to Marc Friedland, manager of Talley's Green Grocery in Charlotte, North Carolina, for his assistance and support. My conversations with Marc over the past few years have been a true education in natural products retailing and have given me tremendous insight into industry trends, values and viewpoints, as well as the challenges and rewards of the natural products retail business. I have developed a deep interest and appreciation for the natural products industry as a result.

Finally, I want to thank my close friends and family for their loving support and kindness. In particular, my parents, Milt and Kay Babich, have made this book possible by giving me the kind of assistance that only a mother and father would be willing to give. I am fortunate to have them in my life, as well as my other family members with whom I am close, and my good friends. It's these relationships that make my work possible, and they add immeasurably to the enjoyment and satisfaction of it. I am very grateful for one and all.

The Natural Kitchen

Part 1

THE BASICS
BEFORE WE GO

1

BEYOND RICE CAKES AND TOFU

Do you remember when rice cakes and tofu could only be found in "health food stores"? Those were the same off-the-beaten-track nooks that catered to the sandals crowd, doubled as command central for activists, smelled like a musty mixture of whole foods and vitamin supplements, and sold fresh sprouts, granola, and soy milk.

That was then. This is now.

Today, your local supermarket stocks an entire wall of rice cakes, and you probably have your choice of several types of tofu. In fact, it's likely that your supermarket has devoted at least one aisle to natural foods. Better yet, like a growing number of stores, it may be integrating numerous natural foods items with mainstream brands throughout the store, selling them side by side.

As for those earthy little health food stores of the past, they're now natural products superstores, as modern and convenient and service-oriented as your neighborhood supermarket—or more so.

"Natural foods" are one of the fastest growing segments

of the American food industry. Just about everybody is beginning to recognize the many advantages of natural foods products compared with their mainstream counterparts. You may have already sampled some of them at your neighborhood supermarket. There are many more, though, that your supermarket hasn't yet started to stock. They're still waiting to be discovered at the natural foods store.

HOW IT ALL GOT STARTED

The natural foods movement was created by consumers who wanted to take responsibility for their own diets and health. They didn't trust the food industry to do that for them, and they wanted more control over their food choices. So, many of these early proponents of natural foods set up small shops and became retailers, developing a whole new category of foods within the food industry.

WHAT'S SO NATURAL ABOUT NATURAL FOODS?

You may have wondered what the term *natural foods* means. There's actually no legal definition. But within the industry, the term *natural* is generally understood to describe foods that have been minimally processed and are as close to their natural state as possible. They are free of artificial flavors, colors, preservatives, and any other additives that do not occur naturally in the food.

Natural bread and cereal products, for instance, are likely to be made with whole grains and contain more fiber, vitamins, and minerals than their refined-grain counterparts. Cereals are usually unsweetened or are minimally sweetened, often with fruit juice rather than refined sugars. Quick bread and cake mixes are often free of hydrogenated fats. Candies contain no artificial flavors or colors. Many products are low in sodium, and all of them are free of such additives as monosodium glutamate and sodium nitrite. Many are made with organically grown ingredients.

Individual natural foods stores have their own sets of standards or criteria by which they order products to sell in their stores. Some stores are strictly vegetarian; others are not. Some sell foods made with refined sugars and/or hydrogenated fats; others don't. What these stores do have in common, however, is that each has a set of standards that excludes most of the foods that are sold in conventional supermarkets. You'll need to read the food labels to be certain of which ingredients are or are not included in products at specific stores.

For people who are health-conscious, natural foods are often a more nutritious choice than mainstream brands, and natural food stores usually offer more options within a particular category. Pasta lovers can find rows of different kinds of whole-grain pastas at the natural foods store, including some made with alternative grains for people who are sensitive to wheat and other common grains. At a regular supermarket, you may be lucky to find even a few packages of whole-grain pasta.

It's true that you can buy natural-style peanut butter at any supermarket these days, but at the natural foods store, you can find cashew butter and almond butter as well. And although many supermarkets now carry soy milk and vegetarian burger patties, the number of brands and varieties is still limited. At the natural foods store, there are dozens from which to choose.

WHAT IS ORGANIC?

At natural foods stores, you'll see fruits and vegetables that are labeled "organic," and you'll find packaged foods and other products that list "organic" ingredients on their labels. What does the term organic mean?

The term *organic* generally means that the food has been grown without the use of synthetic fertilizers and pesticides, using ecologically sound farming practices. To be certified as organic, foods must also be grown in soil that has been free of prohibited substances such as chemical pesticides and herbicides for at least three years.

Until recently, however, there were no national standards defining the term *organic*. Rules for certifying foods as organic varied from state to state, and compliance within the industry was voluntary. Without consistent standards in place, many consumers were left confused about the meaning of the term, and many more were left wondering about the legitimacy of foods that carried the organic label.

Fortunately, as this book is being written, the U.S. Department of Agriculture is establishing rules that will define which products may be labeled organic. These standards are expected to be in place by the 1999 growing season or soon thereafter. The rules as they have been proposed stipulate that:

- The Department of Agriculture's organic seal may be carried only by raw products that are 100 percent organic and processed foods that contain 95 percent organic ingredients. To be called organic, the food must be grown without the use of added hormones, pesticides, or synthetic fertilizers, and the soil in which the food was grown must have been free of these substances for at least three years.

- Processed food containing 50 percent to 95 percent organic ingredients may be labeled "made with certain organic ingredients."

- Products containing less than 50 percent organic ingredients may only use the word *organic* in the list of ingredients on the food label.

Organic growers and packagers lobbied for national organic standards for several years. Many advocates of the standards, however, were unhappy that the proposed rules fell short of addressing issues concerning genetic engineering of plants and animals, food irradiation to kill bacteria, and the use of municipal waste as fertilizer. The federal government considered these concerns to be "new issues" and in need of further debate before they could be settled.

At the time of writing, however, the Department of Agriculture has indicated that it will reconsider these issues in light of the overwhelmingly negative response within the natural foods industry to the proposed standards.

HOW NATURAL DO I HAVE TO BE?

Are natural foods a better choice than mainstream brands? Should I buy organically grown foods and products made with organic ingredients?

THE CHOICE OF NATURAL

I am an advocate of buying and eating foods that are as close to their natural state as possible. Foods in their natural state have no added sugar or salt, no artificial flavorings or colorings, and no artificial preservatives. Also, the more highly processed a food is, the more likely it is that nutrients have been lost and that undesirable ingredients have been added.

I like short ingredient lists on packaged foods, and I avoid foods that contain additives that have not been well tested or have been shown to be of questionable safety. All of these criteria are more reliably and consistently met by foods found in a natural foods store.

Of course, that doesn't mean that some mainstream brands aren't also nutritious and wholesome choices. In fact, there are many mainstream products that are excellent choices. It really comes down to comparing individual products to determine whether they are of comparable or equivalent quality.

As time goes by, neighborhood supermarkets will be integrating even more natural food products into their stores. Hopefully, mainstream food producers will also begin making changes in the production of their own products so that more of them will meet the criteria of current natural food products. Think of how many great choices we'll all have then!

Finally, it should also be pointed out that not all natural foods are without fault or are nutritional powerhouses. Natural cakes, cookies, and candies can contain loads of fat and calories which many people already eat in excess. Granted, the fat may be a healthier form of fat, and the calories may come with added nutrients from whole grains and real fruit sweeteners. When it comes to treats such as these, let's just say that the natural foods brands are generally the best of the worst. More about when being natural isn't enough later.

THE CHOICE OF ORGANIC

The question of whether or not to buy organically grown foods is a bit more complicated.

Nutritionally, organically grown foods do not differ significantly in their value compared with conventionally grown foods. However, it's clear that organically grown foods are a healthier choice when it comes to the issue of dodging environmental contaminants. I try to buy organically grown foods whenever possible in order to minimize my exposure to such environmental hazards as pesticides and herbicides and other residues. Plus, I like the idea of supporting farmers that use environmentally friendly farming methods. Organically grown produce often tastes better, too. In fact, many chefs are beginning to use more organic and natural foods for that reason.

On the other hand, I also weigh the practical consideration of cost. Organically grown foods usually cost more than the regular supermarket varieties. At some regular supermarkets, the choices of organically grown foods are limited, and sometimes the produce itself doesn't look very good. It's at times close to spoiling, because it doesn't sell as quickly as the other foods. Spoilage isn't as likely to be a problem in large natural foods stores, where the sales volumes are greater and turnover is quicker, but for people who don't have access to large natural foods stores, these practical issues can be reasons not to buy organic.

So, sometimes I buy organic and sometimes I don't. If the produce I buy is not organically grown, I am sure to wash it well with a little bit of dish soap and water, and I peel any fruits or vegetables that have a waxy coating. You can also clean fruits and vegetables with one of the commercial produce washes that are now available in spray bottles. They're found in the produce section of the store.

If you live in a small community where you don't have access to a large natural foods store, you might also consider making the effort to buy locally grown fruits and vegetables from farmers' markets and roadside stands in season. It's a nice way to support local farmers, and the produce that you buy is likely to be fresher and of greater nutritional value than the produce that was picked green and shipped across the country to a store the week before.

EAT WELL, STAY WELL

There is another way to look at the issue of buying organic.

If you eat a healthful diet in keeping with today's dietary recommendations, then you eat a diet that consists primarily of fruits, vegetables, and whole-grain breads and cereal products. Some people call this a plant-based diet. In a plant-based diet, animal products such as meats, eggs, and dairy foods play a minor role. They're eaten in very small amounts—as a minor ingredient in a dish or as a condiment—or they're pushed off the plate altogether. The U.S. Department of Agriculture's Food Guide Pyramid below may help you to visualize the major role that grains, fruits, and vegetables play in a healthful diet.

Plant-based diets are high in fiber, and a high-fiber diet decreases the amount of time it takes for food to work its way through the body and out. So, if you eat a high-fiber diet but can't buy organically grown foods, the environmental contaminants found in conventionally grown foods will be less likely to be absorbed and will work their way out of your system more quickly. Fiber also binds with some contaminants and can help to remove them from your system.

Furthermore, plants contain only a small fraction of the amount of contaminants found in animal products. Environmental contaminants are concentrated in animal tissues, especially in fat. If you limit your intake of animal products, you'll reduce your exposure to these substances.

So, whether or not you buy organically grown foods, there's built-in protection if you eat a high-fiber, plant-based diet.

OTHER CONSIDERATIONS

In addition to the general health concerns that motivate people to buy natural foods—weight control, reducing blood

Food Guide Pyramid
A Guide to Daily Food Choices

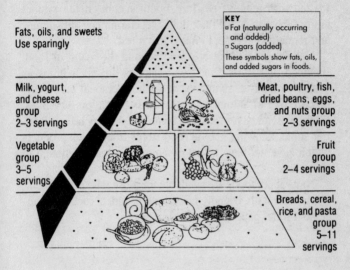

Fats, oils, and sweets
Use sparingly

KEY
▫ Fat (naturally occurring and added)
▫ Sugars (added)
These symbols show fats, oils, and added sugars in foods.

Milk, yogurt, and cheese group
2–3 servings

Meat, poultry, fish, dried beans, eggs, and nuts group
2–3 servings

Vegetable group
3–5 servings

Fruit group
2–4 servings

Breads, cereal, rice, and pasta group
5–11 servings

cholesterol levels and fat intakes, avoidance of environmental contaminants that may increase cancer risk, and as "preventive medicine"—there are other reasons that many people find natural foods products to be especially helpful.

Natural foods stores usually stock plenty of specialty products made for people who have uncommon or complicated food allergies or sensitivities. For instance, people with wheat allergies can find bread made with rice flour or other grains that they can tolerate, and people who are sensitive to sulfites can find dried fruits and wine that are sulfite-free. People who prefer to avoid caffeine can find several brands of caffeine-free, grain-based hot beverages, and vegetarians can find alternatives to products that usually contain animal by-products. For example, vegetarians can buy gelatin substitutes, candies (such as jelly beans and gumdrops) made without gelatin, shredded wheat cereal frosted with gelatin-free glaze, bouillon cubes made without animal flavorings, tofu hot dogs, vegetarian egg substitutes, and rennetless cheese, to name just a few.

Natural products also extend beyond the realm of food. Included at natural food supermarkets are such items as soaps, toothpaste, shampoo, and other personal care items that are free of animal by-products, synthetic preservatives, fragrances, and dyes to which some people may be sensitive. For some, knowing natural food stores often stock products which have not been tested on animals is reason enough to shop there.

Natural pet foods are available for those who prefer them. Environmentally friendly household products such as cleaners and toilet paper are available, too.

2

ANATOMY OF A NATURAL FOODS STORE

Big or small, what will you find in a natural foods store?

Which products are unique and why?

If you've never before set foot in a natural foods store, you're in for some surprises. You'll find as many similarities with a regular supermarket as you will differences. You'll see cereals on the cereal aisle and milk and butter in the refrigerated section, but you'll also see foods and brand names that you've never seen before with names that you may not know how to pronounce. You'll see some nonfood products, too, that you might not expect to see in a super-market—juicers, incense, massage oils, and aromatherapy products, for instance.

You'll notice differences on a more subtle level, too. Fruits and vegetables don't look as shiny and perfect as they do in the regular supermarket. Organically grown produce has blemishes and lacks the uniform look that characterizes supermarket varieties. Product packaging tends toward the "green," as in brown paper wrapping and other environmentally friendly materials. In-store flyers and books and magazines will lean toward philosophical views with which you may not be familiar. You may even notice a bit of a musty aroma in the store—a blend of fresh produce, spices, nutritional supplements, soaps and packaged goods—that has not been covered up by synthetic cleaners and harsh chemicals.

We'll go aisle by aisle into a natural foods supermarket in the following chapters. But for starters, here's what you can expect to find by general categories of products:

DRY GOODS

Dry goods include a wide range of familiar foods, including cereal, flour, cookies and crackers, packaged mixes, snack foods, pasta and pasta sauces, condiments, breakfast bars and sports or energy bars, canned and packaged soups, canned and packaged beans, baby food, and soy milk, rice milk, and other milk alternatives packaged in aseptic containers that don't need refrigeration. This area of the store also includes bottled beverages such as water, tea, fruit juices, and natural soft drinks, and baking supplies such as sugar and carob chips (the natural foods alternative to chocolate chips), egg and fat replacers.

Most of these foods are staples in your household. The difference is that these products adhere to natural foods standards. For instance, mixes are made with whole grains, cookies are made without hydrogenated fats, tomato sauce is made with organically grown tomatoes, and soft drinks are naturally flavored and caffeine-free.

BULK FOODS

Foods sold in bulk bins are popular in natural foods stores. They are an ecologically sound choice, because they reduce packaging, and they can be less expensive than packaged foods. At some stores, you can bring your own containers from home and refill them at the bulk station at a discounted price. Honey, oils, nut butters, and maple syrup, for instance, are often sold this way. Other foods that are sold in bulk include various types of flour, dry beans, peas and lentils, cereal, coffee, instant mixes (such as soup and pancake mixes), rice, nuts, seeds, and pasta.

There are a few drawbacks to foods sold in bulk bins. These concern sanitation issues. Foods in these bins may be exposed to fingers and hands, insect infestation, and germs that can collect on the handles of scoops that may fall into the bins. If you buy from bulk bins, consider whether the bins appears clean, lids are tightly sealed, and scoops are situated in such a way that handles don't touch the food. Foods purchased from bulk bins should be stored in the refrigerator or freezer to discourage the growth of moths.

REFRIGERATED FOODS

At first glance, this section may look like the dairy case in any supermarket, but look a little closer and you'll see big differences. For starters, the milk is often hormone-free, meaning it comes from cows that have not been treated with BST, or bovine growth hormone. The butter may be organic and is naturally colored, that is, more white than yellow. Cheese is often rennet-free (rennet is an enzyme used in cheese making that comes from the stomach lining of calves). If yogurt products are sweetened, they may be sweetened with honey or fruit juice rather than corn syrup or processed cane sugar.

You'll find soy alternatives to dairy products here, such as fresh soy milk, soy yogurt, and soy cheese. This section is where you'll find tofu and tempeh and vegetarian meat substitutes for cold cuts, burger patties, hot dogs, and sausage. You'll also see fresh tortillas and some specialty foods such as fresh miso (a fermented soy product) and certain other products that are free of preservatives and need refrigeration.

FROZEN FOODS

Some of the same foods found in the refrigerated section can also be found in the frozen food cases, such as some meat substitutes and breads. You'll also see frozen entrées here, including ethnic dinners. You'll see ice cream, dairy-free frozen desserts, and other frozen novelties. You'll also find packages of frozen, organically grown vegetables and fruits.

This section tends to have a little bit of everything that you would ordinarily find in the regular supermarket. The selection is not extensive, but it's growing rapidly. In a regular supermarket, for instance, you might see numerous types of frozen waffles—in the natural foods store, you're likely to find one or two brands. In some regular supermarkets, you'll find an entire aisle of freezer cases devoted to frozen entrées. In the natural foods store, you'll find a few dozen choices. That includes dinners as well as snack foods such as individually wrapped frozen burritos and frozen pizzas.

THE DELI AND PREPARED FOODS

Most natural foods stores have a refrigerator case for ready-to-eat prepared foods such as sandwiches, salads, dips and spreads, and freshly squeezed juice drinks. Some sell an extensive selection of these items in a deli area. The deli area may also include a soup and salad bar, and if the store has a café area, it may serve hot items such as stir-fries, veggie burgers, and other entrées. Juice bars and smoothies are also becoming common.

THE BAKERY

Natural foods bakery areas carry bagels, muffins, and breads made with whole-grain flours and without synthetic preservatives. Cakes, cookies, and other baked goods are made without hydrogenated shortening and contain natural fillings and flavorings. Some of the products may be made locally or on-site. Whether they're made in the store kitchen or not, you can usually be sure that the food is fresh, because the lack of preservatives in these products means that the shelf life is relatively short.

NONFOOD PRODUCTS

Natural foods stores are actually more accurately termed natural *products* stores, since they carry much more than just food. This book focuses on food choices at natural product supermarkets. However, you'll be interested to know that these stores carry many interesting nonfood products as well.

PERSONAL CARE ITEMS

Traditional shampoos, soaps, lotions, cosmetics, toothpaste, mouthwash, and other personal care products usually contain such ingredients as mineral oil, synthetic fragrances and dyes, petroleum, and chemical preservatives. Some people are allergic or sensitive to some of these ingredients or wish to avoid them for other reasons. Traditional versions of these products are often tested on animals, or they contain animal by-products such as lanolin or tallow, which many vegetarians choose to avoid. Natural counterparts to these products are free of these ingredients.

HOUSEHOLD GOODS

Household cleaners and paper goods tend to be produced using ingredients that are often (but not always) less environmentally toxic, and the packaging tends to be more environmentally friendly. For instance, laundry soaps may be phosphate-free, and sprays may not contain fluorocarbons and other propellants.

In very large natural products stores, you may also find clothing, appliances such as juicers and coffeemakers, and kitchen supplies and utensils.

PET FOOD

Natural pet food is made following much the same standards as other natural food products. Canned and dry food and treats are made without synthetic coloring, flavoring, dyes, and fillers. Some of these products are also free of animal by-products, so they are more acceptable to some vegetarians.

BOOKS AND MAGAZINES

Natural foods stores usually have a commitment to consumer education, so they often have a good-sized area devoted to books and magazines on subjects ranging from yoga, meditation, and massage to alternative medicine and nutrition, among others. They usually carry an assortment of vegetarian cookbooks and other guides to using whole foods.

MEAT

Natural foods stores sell a wide range of vegetarian products and meat alternatives. However, for people who include meat, poultry, and seafood in their diets, the natural foods store sells products that come from animals that have not been fed hormones or antibiotics. The meat may also come from animals that have lived their lives in more humane living environments that allowed more freedom of movement compared with animals raised on factory farms.

WINE, COFFEE, AND GOURMET FOODS

In states that permit supermarkets to sell alcoholic beverages, large natural foods stores carry a selection of wines that have been made without sulfites and with organically grown grapes. Organic coffee and tea are also available. Some stores also carry other gourmet and specialty foods that are made in keeping with generally accepted "natural" standards.

3
USING THE FOOD GUIDE

The purpose of this book is to introduce beginners—those of you who may never before have set foot in a natural foods store—to products that will be useful in helping you live a healthier lifestyle. These are products that you'll truly enjoy using. Rather than describing each and every product available (there are thousands), this book points out some of the best, most convenient, tasty, and healthful foods available— great starter foods for beginners.

This book's organization takes its cue from natural foods stores themselves, so foods are grouped just as you'll find them in most stores. The tour takes you aisle by aisle through the store, pointing out some particularly great products along the way, some of which are excellent substitutes for their less healthy counterparts in the traditional supermarket. Nutrition information is given for these foods, along with explanations of how to use them and quick and easy recipes and serving ideas.

WHEN BEING NATURAL ISN'T ENOUGH

Of course, just because a food is natural doesn't mean it's a nutritional powerhouse. Being natural also doesn't always mean that a particular food is better than its supermarket counterpart.

Although the primary emphasis of this book is the many great choices at natural foods stores, I'll also point out examples of natural foods that you might have thought were a good idea but that, in fact, don't deserve a second glance.

GETTING STARTED: THE BEGINNER'S TOP-TEN LIST

If you read no further in this book, or to kick off your foray into natural foods, read the "don't miss" list that follows. It will tip you off to ten of the most nutritious, practical, and versatile food products found in natural foods supermarkets. More detailed information about each of these is included later in the book, along with descriptions of many more foods that you'll want to try.

1. Soy Milk

For anyone who is lactose-intolerant or prefers to avoid dairy products, this is a super-nutritious alternative to cow's milk. For everyone else, it's a good sense product that is nutritious and packed with health-supporting phytochemicals, substances found in foods of plant origin that may provide health benefits. It tastes great and comes plain and in different flavors. Use it cup for cup in any recipe that calls for milk, or drink it straight. Packaged in aseptic, shelf-stable boxes, it needs no refrigeration until you open it.

2. Powdered Vegetarian Egg Replacer

A one-pound box of this product will last you two years or longer. It takes the place of eggs in virtually any recipe that calls for them and works wonderfully. A mixture of vegetable starches, it's cholesterol- and saturated-fat-free.

3. Vegetarian Burger Patties

There's a huge variety to suit anyone's taste preferences. Quick and convenient, they blow away their real meat counterparts in terms of health and nutrition. And everyone loves the way they taste. They're great as a quick meal for teens or anyone who doesn't have time to cook. Take them to picnics and cookouts.

4. Whole-Grain Cold Breakfast Cereals

If you're tired of the same old same old, put a few of these into your basket for a nice change of pace. They're whole grain so they're an excellent source of fiber and minerals, and they're free of hydrogenated fats. These aren't for adults only, either. There are fun versions for kids, too. Oh, and they taste great.

5. Tofu

Don't laugh. Tofu is versatile. Forget tofu burgers and stir-fry—tofu has many more surprising uses. It takes the place of eggs in some recipes, and it takes the place of dairy products in others. Quiche, sandwich fillings, pudding and pie fillings, whipped topping, dips and sauces—tofu works marvelously in all of these dishes and more.

6. Organic Canned Beans

This is one of the most convenient products around. If you have canned beans in your cupboard, you always have something to make for dinner. Add them to soups and salads, mash them for dips and spreads, toss them with pasta, or heat them and eat them plain with a scoop of salsa. They taste great, they're fast, and they're nutritious. Beans are fiber superstars.

7. Dried Bean Flakes

You probably haven't seen these in the regular supermarket yet. If you have trouble finding them at the natural foods store, look a little harder—they're probably hidden among the soup mixes. Find them. Like canned beans, they're quick and convenient. Just add hot water, and in five minutes you've got a smooth, hot bean dip or filling for your burritos or tacos. They come in pinto bean or black bean varieties.

8. Whole-Grain Mixes

Just like their traditional counterparts in the regular supermarket—pancake and waffle mixes, quick bread mixes, and rice and couscous side dishes. The difference is they don't contain the hydrogenated fats, unnecessary additives, and refined flours.

9. Instant Soups

The cup-of-soup kind. Just add hot water and you've got soup or chili in its own little bowl. Practical for at home, at work, even for trips in the car. These are the forerunners of the mainstream brand knockoffs, but they're better for you. They usually have far less sodium, and they're made with organically grown ingredients and whole grains.

10. Organic Canned Tomatoes

Tomatoes tend to be treated heavily with pesticides and herbicides when they are grown conventionally, so buying organically grown canned tomato products makes good sense. Plus, regular canned tomatoes are high in sodium. Many of the brands found in natural foods stores have no salt added. Canned tomatoes are a staple ingredient in many stews, casseroles, soups, sauces, and numerous other dishes.

And there you have it—the starting lineup. For even more great choices, read on.

Part 2

LET'S GO SHOPPING!

FRESH STARTS BEGIN HERE: THE PRODUCE SECTION

TODAY'S FEATURES: KALE, SWISS CHARD, BOK CHOY, MANGO, PAPAYA, SWEET POTATO, OTHERS

Whether I'm giving a tour of a regular supermarket or a natural foods store, I usually start here, in the produce section. True, it's the first area you're likely to see when you enter the store. But that's not the primary reason I like to begin here.

The produce section is the most important area in any food store, because this is where you will find the foods that are the freshest and most healthful—foods in their natural state. These foods make up the backbone of the healthiest diet. Most natural foods stores carry a mix of organic and conventionally grown produce. Since much of the produce is organic, fruits and vegetables will have a blemish or two. That's a small price to pay for the loads of fiber, vitamins, minerals, and health-protecting phytochemicals they provide, and the environmental contaminants that you'll avoid. This is the place to fill up your basket.

If you are like many people, though, you may balk at

"filling up your basket" with fruits and vegetables. Why? Here are two possibilities:

Fresh fruits and vegetables mean work. For some people, the produce area spells "washing, chopping, peeling"—in other words, a lot of time. Time that they don't have to devote to fixing a meal.

In this chapter, I'll show you some fast fresh foods and give you some tips for cutting down on kitchen time.

Habit. Let's face it. For many folks, a trip to the produce area means making a beeline for the iceberg lettuce, tomatoes, and bananas. Then they're outta there.

If that describes you, maybe it's time to broaden your gustatory horizons. Where food is concerned, the variety is in the plant world. The best way to add variety in color, flavor, texture, and aroma to your diet—not to mention nutrition—is to increase the number of different kinds of fruits and vegetables that you eat and to learn to prepare them in interesting and satisfying ways.

In this chapter, I'll introduce you to some fruits and vegetables that may be new to you and suggest some quick and easy ways to enjoy them.

Fresh fruits and vegetables are excellent sources of disease-fighting phytochemicals that may protect you against coronary artery disease and some forms of cancer. Many health organizations now urge everyone to eat at least five servings or more of fruits or vegetables per day. Count one medium piece of fruit, a half cup of juice, a half cup of cooked fruit or vegetable, or one cup raw as one serving. Instead of thinking of these foods as side dishes with your meals, think of them as main courses. Think large servings. When you eat broccoli, carrots, greens, and fruit salad, take a heaping helping—one cup or more.

THE ALL-STAR LINEUP

In this chapter, I've promised to introduce you to some fruits and vegetables with which you may not be familiar. I've chosen several, but they are merely a representative sample of what's actually available.

The best way to get familiar with new foods is to experiment. The next time you go shopping, take an extra five or ten minutes in the produce section to carefully examine what's available. Stop and look at some of the foods that you've previously passed up, then buy one that you've never before tried. When you try new foods, you're likely to come upon a dud now and then. But over time, if you make a habit of experimenting with new foods, you'll find many new favorites.

Are there some fruits and vegetables that are better for you than others? The answer is a qualified yes.

Generally, the most nutrient-dense fruits and vegetables are those that are deep yellow, deep orange or red, or deep green in color. The color is the giveaway that these foods have the most vitamins, minerals, and health-enhancing phytochemicals compared with other foods. (There are some exceptions, of course, such as cauliflower, which is white in color but super-nutritious.) They tend to be rich in vitamins A and C, folic acid, iron, and calcium, as well as phytochemicals such as carotenoids and lycopene, to name only two of the hundreds, and possibly thousands, that exist.

Carrots, tomatoes, sweet potatoes, kale, mustard greens, turnip greens, peaches, and apricots, for instance, are all deep yellow, red, or green in color. They are far more nutritious than, say, celery, mushrooms, eggplant, or iceberg lettuce, which lack the same rich coloring *(see When Being Natural Isn't Enough, page 43)*. That doesn't mean that the latter don't have some nutritional merit or shouldn't be enjoyed as part of your diet. It's just that, cup for cup, those in the first list are considerably more nutritious. They're the superstars of the plant kingdom.

A partial list of fresh fruit and vegetable "nutritional superstars" follows. Use this list and the specific examples that follow in this chapter to inspire you to eat more of these foods every day.

Consider These Nutritional Superstars

Acorn Squash	Brussels Sprouts	Kale	Spinach
Apricots	Cabbage	Mangoes	Sweet Potatoes
Arugula	Cantaloupe	Oranges	Swiss Chard
Bell Peppers	Cauliflower	Papayas	Tomatoes
Bok Choy	Collards	Peaches	Watermelon
Broccoli	Grapefruit		

• KAY'S BROCCOLI SALAD •

My mother's broccoli salad is addictive. You might as well double the recipe, because you won't be able to stop eating it. This is a pretty salad to take to parties or serve to guests. You can substitute cauliflower for broccoli or mix the two.

1 bunch of broccoli florets
1 cup dried cherries
1 sweet onion, diced
½ cup salted sunflower seeds
½ cup soy mayonnaise (see Aisle 4)
2 tablespoons red wine vinegar
¼ cup sugar

Combine the first 4 ingredients in a large bowl. Whisk together the mayonnaise, vinegar, and sugar in a separate bowl and pour this dressing over the other ingredients. Toss well to coat, then chill.

Yield: About 4 good-sized servings (1 cup each). Of course, that depends on your definition of a serving. For me, this recipe makes only 2 servings. That's why I double it.

Nutritional content per one-cup serving: Calories (Kcal): 348, Protein (gm): 8.5, Total fat (gm): 16, Saturated fat (gm): 1, Cholesterol (mg): 0, Dietary fiber (gm): 4, Sodium (mg): 343, Calcium (mg): 88, Iron (mg): 3, Zinc (mg): 1, Vitamin A (I.U.): 1,610, Vitamin C (mg): 86

KALE

What Is It?

You've seen it; you just might not realize that you've seen it. Kale is that dark, blue-green leafy stuff that you most often see as a garnish around restaurant salad bars. It's thick and rubbery, so it happens to hold up well sitting out on a buffet line all day.

Sad to say, that's how most people have come to know kale. If you ever taste cooked kale, though, you'll love it. It also happens to be incredibly nutritious.

Though they don't look much alike, kale is similar in flavor to broccoli. No wonder—they're both members of the large cabbage family, which includes bok choy or Chinese cabbage, brussels sprouts, collard greens, mustard greens, turnip greens, cauliflower, kohlrabi, daikon, radishes, watercress, and arugula (a peppery-tasting green that is often included in salad green mixtures).

How Can I Use It?

Kale is delicious as a cooked vegetable. It's fast and easy to fix. You can also chop it and add it to soups, gratins, and casseroles. Kale is delicious, for instance, sliced into strips and stirred into white bean soup or mixed into a potato gratin.

Most often, I just eat it steamed with a little olive oil and garlic. I pour a teaspoon or two of olive oil onto the bottom of a skillet and add a half teaspoon of minced garlic and a quarter cup of water. Add several large leaves of chopped kale, cover the skillet, and on medium heat steam the kale for several minutes, until the kale is softened.

Serving Other Greens

After you've tried kale, experiment with other greens as well. Mustard greens, spinach, Swiss chard, turnip greens, and collard greens can often be used interchangeably in recipes. I like to stir leftover cooked spinach into lentil soup. You can also mix chopped, cooked greens into lasagna filling, or serve them over a plate of fettuccine. In the South, cooked, mixed greens are served with a splash of vinegar or hot pepper sauce on top. Braised greens with garlic and soy sauce are good, too.

Nutritional Features

Like other leafy greens, kale is rich in iron, calcium, vitamins A and C, and folic acid. Recent research has shown that the calcium found in kale is absorbed as well as or slightly better than the calcium that is present in cow's milk. It's a very smart move to include large servings of dark green, leafy vegetables in your diet often. Here's a nutritional comparison of several:

Nutrients in One Cup of Cooked Greens.

(Source: *Food Values of Portions Commonly Used*, 15th edition, by Jean Pennington, HarperPerennial, 1989)

	Kale	Swiss Chard	Collard	Mustard
Calories (Kcal):	42	36	54	22
Protein (gm):	2.4	3.4	4.2	3.2
Iron (mg):	1.2	1.1	1.6	1.0
Calcium (mg):	94	78	296	104
Vitamin A (I.U.):	9,620	5,524	8,436	4,244
Vitamin C (mg):	54	32	38	36
Folic Acid (mcg):	18	N/A	24	N/A

Buying and Storing Kale

Kale is sold in bunches or loose leaves. When you choose greens, choose leaves that are about the size of an adult's hand, or not more than about eight to ten inches in length. Larger leaves may be too tough; smaller, younger leaves are more tender and have a better texture. When you prepare kale, you'll need to cut off the tough stem that extends up into the leaf.

Store kale in the refrigerator. Kale keeps longer than many salad greens, but it's best to use it within four or five days or it will begin to spoil. I like to wrap leaves in a dampened sheet of paper toweling, then store them in a large airtight plastic bag or container. You can also store the kale in the vegetable crisper in the refrigerator. If I have more kale than I can use before it spoils, I cook all of it at one time. Then I save the cooked leftovers in the refrigerator and add them to soup or eat them over rice or pasta over the next day or two.

• BRAISED KALE AND SESAME •

One bunch of kale (about 6 cups chopped)
1 teaspoon sesame oil or olive oil
1 teaspoon minced garlic
1 tablespoon toasted sesame seeds
½ cup water

Rinse the kale leaves well, remove the thick stems, and set aside. Pour oil onto bottom of a skillet, add minced garlic, and cook on low heat for 1–2 minutes, stirring occasionally to keep garlic from sticking. Add water and heat until steaming.

Add kale leaves and sesame seeds. Cover the skillet with a lid and cook on medium heat for 3–5 minutes until tender.

Yield: About 2 cups cooked kale.

Nutritional content per ½ cup serving*: Calories (Kcal): 52, Total Fat (gm): 3, Saturated Fat (gm): 0.4, Cholesterol (mg): 0, Dietary Fiber (gm): 3, Vitamin A (I.U.): 4,810, Vitamin C (mg): 27, Folic Acid (mcg): 9, Sodium (mg): 16, Calcium (mg): 83, Iron (mg): 1.1

When you bring groceries home, get into the habit of taking ten or fifteen minutes to wash, peel, and chop fresh vegetables—broccoli, cauliflower, carrots, onions—and store them in an airtight container in the refrigerator. They'll be ready to steam or stir-fry the next time you prepare a meal. Having a few fresh items preprepared can make the difference between working them into your diet or not, especially during the week when schedules can be hectic.

*Doubling the portion size to one cup is a great idea.

It's also fine to buy some preprepared fresh foods. You'll pay more if someone peels your carrots for you, but the extra cost can be worth it if it makes the difference between eating those foods or not. Prewashed, mixed salad greens, cut vegetables, cored pineapples, and peeled baby carrots are examples.

• **SWEET CARROT ORANGE DRINK** •

Many natural foods stores stock freshly squeezed fruit and vegetable juices, which are delicious and highly nutritious. Try mixing fresh carrot juice with fresh orange juice—a wonderful blend!

¾ cup freshly squeezed orange juice
¼ cup fresh carrot juice

Pour carrot juice into a tall glass, then add orange juice. Stir and enjoy.

Makes 1 cup.

Nutrient content: Calories (Kcal): 108, Protein (gm): 0.5, Total fat (gm): 0, Saturated fat (gm): 0, Cholesterol (mg): 0, Dietary fiber (gm): 3, Sodium (mg): 20, Calcium (mg): 35, Iron (mg): 1, Zinc (mg): 0.2, Vitamin A (I.U.): 16,209, Vitamin C (mg): 98

SWEET POTATO

What Is It?

Okay, so you know what a sweet potato is. But do you know the difference between a sweet potato and a yam?

A sweet potato is the thick, sweet tuberous root of a tropical vine that is related to the morning glory. This root is nutritionally very rich. Sweet potatoes are moist and deep orange in color, so not surprisingly, they're a terrific source of vitamin A and carotenoids, as well as vitamin C and potassium. In the United States, sweet potatoes are a traditional Southern crop. If you've lived or traveled in the American South, you may have tried sweet potato pie or sweet potato casserole.

Yams are related to sweet potatoes. Like sweet potatoes, they come from the roots of tropical vines and are a starchy, staple food in the areas where they grow. True yams are much paler in color than sweet potatoes, and they contain only a small amount of vitamin A and a much smaller amount of vitamin C. Their texture is drier, too. Both are nutritious, worthwhile vegetables, but sweet potatoes are the nutritional all-stars. The American yam sold in the U.S. is actually a sweet potato. Confused? When you have the choice, just remember to buy the deepest-orange-colored vegetable that the store sells. That will be the most nutritious choice.

How Can I Use It?

Sweet potatoes are much too good and much too nutritious to be eaten only once a year for Thanksgiving.

You can fix sweet potatoes almost any way that you fix white potatoes. They can be boiled, mashed, baked, and stuffed. Since they're sweet, they go especially well with fruit. So, topping them with crushed pineapple or orange marmalade, sprinkling them with grated orange or lemon rind and cinnamon, or cooking them with apples, bananas, raisins, or apricots are all delicious ways to fix sweet potatoes.

• CALYPSO SWEET POTATO •

One of my favorite, quick meals is a sweet potato cooked in the microwave oven. It takes next to no time at all, and it satisfies my sweet tooth. I may eat this with a slice or two of whole wheat toast or a mixed green salad. I never tire of it.

One large sweet potato, unpeeled
1 tablespoon brown sugar
Juice from ½ of a fresh lime (about 2 tablespoons of lime juice)

Wash the sweet potato and cut off the 2 ends with a paring knife. Pierce in 2 or 3 places with a fork, then place on a dish and cook uncovered in a microwave oven for 7 or 8 minutes, until soft (test it with a fork).

Slice the potato lengthwise and fold open into 2 halves. Sprinkle with brown sugar, then squeeze fresh lime juice over the top.

Yield: 1 serving (the nutritional content is approximately double that listed in the table on page 38).

Nutritional Features
Remember, deep orange sweet potatoes are nutritional powerhouses. Following is the nutritional breakdown for a half cup of mashed sweet potatoes. Doubling that portion size to a full cup—a good habit to get into whenever you eat fresh fruits and vegetables—would catapult the nutritional contribution of this food into the stratosphere. Who needs vitamin mineral supplements when we have foods as good for you and good tasting as sweet potatoes?

Nutrients in ½ cup of Mashed Sweet Potato

(Source: *Food Values of Portions Commonly Used*)

Calories (Kcal):	172
Protein (gm):	2.7
Vitamin A (I.U.):	27,968
Vitamin C (mg):	28
Folic Acid (mcg):	18
Potassium (mg):	301
Calcium (mg):	35
Iron (mg):	0.92

Buying and Storing Sweet Potatoes

Store fresh sweet potatoes in a cool, dry place, but try to use them within a few days of buying. Sweet potatoes do not keep as well as white potatoes and begin to shrivel and pit fairly quickly. For that reason, it's best to buy only what you are going to use for a meal or two, rather than buying larger quantities as you might when you buy white potatoes.

....

Mashed bananas can be used as an egg substitute in recipes for pancakes, muffins, and cookies—anything in which you wouldn't mind a little banana flavor. Use half of a large, ripe, mashed banana (or one whole small banana) in place of one egg.

....

MANGO AND PAPAYA

What Are They? How Can I Use Them?

When mangoes and papayas became more commonplace in American supermarkets and natural foods stores several years ago, they were often jumbled together in the same bin. There may have been signs indicating the name of the fruit and the price, but you often couldn't tell which item was which. These were fruits that I had never tried before, and they somehow looked alike to me. When I finally mustered the courage to try what I thought was a papaya, I was actually eating a mango. Other people have told me the same story; at least I wasn't alone.

I've got it straight now, and I'm a big fan of both fruits.

Mangoes are native to the East Indies, but they are grown in Florida and California now as well. They're somewhat almond-shaped—big and oval, about six or eight inches in length—with a long, flat pit inside. When mangoes are ripe, they are green and yellow and often red in some areas. They may have some black flecks as well. A ripe mango "gives" a little when squeezed, like an avocado, but it's not mushy. When you find them in the store, they are often hard and green and need to ripen some more before they'll taste good.

Mangoes are delicious; they taste somewhat peachy and have a texture similar to a peach as well. They need to be peeled, which can take some practice. Expect to get a little bit messy the first time you eat a mango. It can be hard to maneuver around the pit *(see How to Eat a Mango below)*. Add chunks of mango to your cereal, to fruit salads, or eat it plain. Some people like to make sorbet or puree with mangoes. Chutney, an Indian relish, is traditionally made with mangoes.

How to Eat a Mango

The greatest challenge in eating a mango is keeping your hands clean—mangoes are messy! Equip yourself with several napkins. Using the following technique can help minimize your need to touch the fruit:

1. Wash the mango.
2. Using a sharp knife, cut the mango in half lengthwise, being careful to work your way around the large, flat

pit that lies in the center. When you are finished, you'll have one small half of the mango and another larger half containing the pit.

3. Cut the pit out of the larger half of the mango.

4. One at a time, hold each mango half in the palm of your hand with the peel touching your hand and the fruit inside facing upward. Using a sharp knife, carefully score each half, crisscrossing the cuts so that each half has been cut into cubes down to but not cutting through the peel.

5. Put down the knife. With two hands, hold the sides of the mango half and turn it inside out. The fruit cubes should push away from the peel, fanning out so that you can take bites without getting mango all over your face. Alternately you can cut the cubes off the skin. Neatly cubed mango makes a great addition to a mixed green salad.

In contrast to the oval-shaped mango, papayas are shaped more like pears or avocados. One end is narrower than the other. You may wonder how people get the two fruits mixed up, but they're often about the same size, and they're often green in the store. Ripe papayas are yellow and green and are soft to the touch, like a ripe peach or pear. Papayas can actually grow to be quite large, however, depending upon the variety. Some Mexican papayas are as big as melons. When I was traveling in Australia, the papayas (which are called pawpaws there) in the supermarkets were very big and were sold by the pound. In the United States, the smaller fruits are more common and are priced per piece.

Like mangoes, papayas are sweet and delicious and bright orange yellow inside. Unlike mangoes, however, which have a big, cumbersome pit inside, papayas have lots of round black seeds in the middle that are easy to scoop out. Some people use these seeds as a garnish or eat them as is, but most of us in the U.S. throw them away and just eat the flesh of the fruit.

Papayas are easy to slice in half. Scoop out the seeds, peel them, and slice the fruit lengthwise. Add pieces of papaya to salads or eat them plain. In the South Pacific, I saw papayas eaten with fresh lime juice squeezed on top for a sweet-tart flavor.

Unripe, green papayas can be used as a vegetable in stir-fry along with other vegetables or cubes of tofu. Shredded green papayas can also be used in salads. You can find spicy green papaya salad, made with shredded papaya, ground peanuts, and spices in some Thai restaurants.

Buying and Storing Mangoes and Papayas

As I described above, mangoes and papayas often come into stores hard and green and underripe. Ripe mangoes should be partly yellow and may have orange, red, and black areas. A ripe papaya has some yellow areas. When ripe, both are slightly soft to the touch but not mushy.

If you buy a green mango or papaya, set it out on a windowsill or on your kitchen counter for a day or two until it softens a bit. You can also set it inside a paper bag, which will ripen the fruit more quickly.

If you don't eat ripe mangoes and papayas right away, store them in the refrigerator to keep them from spoiling. They'll only keep in the refrigerator for a few days, though. Eat them as soon as possible.

• JAMAICAN BREAKFAST SALAD •

If you have too much fruit on hand and it's all ripening at the same time, cut it up and make fruit salad. Somehow, fruit salad always seems to disappear more quickly than plain fresh fruit. Here's an easy recipe for a sunny salad that goes well with muffins in the morning.

1 cup papaya, cut into cubes
1 cup mango, cut into cubes
1 cup banana slices
Juice of 1 freshly squeezed lime (about ¼ cup)

Optional: if you have pineapple on hand, add up to 1 cup of pineapple chunks.

Combine all ingredients and chill.

Yield: 6 half-cup servings.

Nutritional content per ½ cup serving: Calories (Kcal): 52, Total fat (gm): 0, Saturated fat (gm): 0, Cholesterol (mg): 0, Dietary fiber (gm): 1, Sodium (mg): 1, Calcium (mg): 11, Iron (mg): 0.1, Vitamin A (I.U.): 1,830, Vitamin C (mg): 29

Nutritional Features
Mangoes and papayas are excellent sources of vitamins A and C and potassium. They're good sources of niacin, and papayas are also a good source of calcium.

Nutrients in One Medium Piece of Fruit

(Source: *Food Values of Portions Commonly Used*)

	Mango	**Papaya**
Calories (Kcal):	135	117
Vitamin A (I.U.):	8,060	6,122
Vitamin C (mg):	57	188
Niacin (mg):	1.2	1.0
Potassium (mg):	322	780
Calcium (mg):	21	72

WHEN BEING NATURAL ISN'T ENOUGH

In the beginning of this section, I said that the most nutrient-dense fruits and vegetables are those that are deep green or deep orange or red in color. These rich colors are clues that the foods contain large amounts of vitamins, minerals, and phytochemicals, such as vitamin A, vitamin C, iron, calcium, and carotenoids such as beta-carotene and lycopene. Go out of your way to eat such foods often.

You might also like to know that there are some fruits and vegetables that have relatively little nutritional value. Some of these may surprise you.

Whether they come from a natural foods store or not, these foods have little value nutritionally: mushrooms (including the popular portobello), celery, eggplant, cucumbers, iceberg lettuce, and cherries. There are certainly others, but the point is that even among those foods that are generally the most healthful, there are wide variations in nutritional value.

There's no need to avoid these foods, but you also don't need to go out of your way to include them in your diet. Let's call them "nutritional neutrals," since they'll neither hurt your nor help you. Given a choice, the superstars that

I listed earlier are a much better nutritional bargain. Later in this book, I will, however, point out some natural products that are simply natural versions of junk foods. These are the foods that you really are best off avoiding or eating infrequently.

AISLE I BULK

GRAIN	NUTS
FLOUR	HONEY
SEEDS	BEANS

TODAY'S FEATURES:
AMARANTH, KAMUT, QUINOA, SPELT, AND TEFF

You're familiar with the usual lineup: wheat, rice, rye, oats, corn, barley—maybe you've even cooked with buckwheat. These are the grains and flours that have been widely used in Western countries for centuries. Now it's time to meet some newcomers that are just as delicious and nutritious but haven't quite made it into mainstream supermarkets . . . yet. You'll find these in the natural foods store, and they're worth getting to know.

UNCOMMON GRAINS WORTH TRYING

AMARANTH

What Is It?

Amaranth is an ancient grain; it was a staple food of the Aztecs in Central America. It grows as a broad-leafed plant that produces tens of thousands of little seeds about the size of a poppy seed. Amaranth is sold as a whole grain or flour, and you'll see it listed as an ingredient in commercial breakfast cereals and crackers sold in natural foods stores.

How Can I Use It?

Use amaranth flour to bake breads, muffins or biscuits, cakes, crackers, pancakes, and other baked goods. It can also be used to make pasta. Amaranth has a distinctive flavor, which has been described as "slightly peppery" as well as "mild and sweet" and "mild and nutty," depending upon the variety. So, you may want to experiment with recipes to see which ones taste best using this grain. You may even want to mix amaranth with other grains.

While you're at it, stock some millet in your cupboard as well. Millet is the familiar little round, yellow seed that is commonly used as bird food, though the millet that is sold for human consumption has had the outer hull removed. Add a handful of millet to muffin and bread recipes for extra crunch and pretty yellow flecks of color. That's about a quarter cup of millet per two dozen muffins or one loaf of bread.

If you use amaranth to make yeast breads, you'll have to mix it with another flour in order for the bread to rise, since amaranth is low in gluten. Gluten is a protein that gives yeast breads a structure that traps the gases produced by the yeast and allows the bread to rise. Insufficient or low-quality gluten causes the structure of the bread to be weak, resulting in bread that can't hold its shape and turns out dense and low in volume.

Amaranth seeds are the intact grain. You can cook these and use them in many of the same ways that you might use rice—in casseroles, topped with vegetable mixtures, as a cooked side dish, or in pilaf. Cooked amaranth can also be eaten as a hot cereal or combined with other grains as a mixed-grain hot cereal. Amaranth seeds can also be popped and eaten similarly to popcorn, or they can be toasted.

Basic Instructions for Cooking Grains

Grains can generally be used interchangeably in recipes. So, if you don't happen to have a particular type of grain for the recipe you want to make, or if you want to use up a grain that you've had on hand for a long time, you can swap one for another. Out of rice? Use barley. Have you had a box of quinoa in the refrigerator for months? Use it in place of rice in a pilaf.

Grain	Water/Vegetable broth (cups)	Cooking Time	Yield (cups)
1 cup			
Amaranth	3	25 minutes	3
Kamut	1½	1 hour	2½
Quinoa	3	20 minutes	3
Spelt	2	1½ hours	3
Teff	4	15–20 minutes	3

Note: to cook grains, bring the water or vegetable broth to a boil in a saucepan, then add the grain. Reduce the heat, cover the pan, then simmer for the suggested cooking time above or until the liquid is absorbed. If you are rushed for time, you can also pour the boiling liquid over the grain, stir, cover the pan, then take the pan off the heat and let it set for a few hours. In most cases, the grain will gradually absorb the fluid. Fluff the grain with a fork and reheat in a microwave oven or nonstick pan before serving. Cooked grains can keep in the refrigerator for about one week in an airtight container.

QUINOA

What Is It?

Quinoa (pronounced "KEEN-wah") is a high-protein grain that was used by the Incas in Peru and is now popular around the world because of its nutritional value and pleasant flavor. Like amaranth, quinoa is not a true cereal grain. It's the fruit of a plant rather than a grass. Nevertheless, it is treated as a grain in cooking. Quinoa grains are tiny and flat and range in color from white or yellow to dark brown.

In its natural state, quinoa is coated with saponin, a substance found on some plants, which lathers when wet and is slightly toxic. Packaged quinoa is washed free of saponin, but it may be necessary to check with your store manager if you buy bulk quinoa to be sure that you don't have to wash it before using. You may want to rinse it again anyway. Quinoa is sold in its whole form and is also used in combination with other grains in commercial breakfast cereals sold in natural foods stores.

How Can I Use It?

Quinoa can be cooked and used like rice and other cooked grains in casseroles, salads, as an accompaniment or side dish with cooked vegetables and other dishes, and so on. It can also be toasted to give it a nuttier flavor.

• QUINOA-VEGETABLE PILAF •

½ cup quinoa
2 teaspoons olive oil
½ cup chopped onions
1 cup vegetable broth

1 cup grated carrots
¾ cup sliced rutabaga or kolrabi
½ cup diced zucchini
½ cup diced yellow squash
½ teaspoon salt, or to taste

1. Place the quinoa in a large bowl; fill bowl with cool water and then drain into a strainer. Repeat 4 more times or until the water no longer looks soapy.
2. In a 1½ quart saucepan, melt the butter or margarine over medium-high heat. Add the onions; cook, stirring, until softened, about 2 minutes. Add the quinoa; cook, stirring until quinoa makes popping sounds, about 1 to 2 minutes. Add the broth and bring to a boil.
3. Add the carrots, rutabaga, zucchini, and salt. Reduce heat and simmer, covered, 15 minutes or until the liquid is absorbed.

Makes 3 cups.

Nutrient content per ½ cup serving: Calories (Kcal): 40, Protein (gm): 1, Total fat (gm): 2, Saturated fat (gm): 1, Cholesterol (mg): 5, Dietary fiber (gm): 1, Sodium (mg): 185, Calcium (mg): 25, Iron (mg): 0, Zinc (mg): 0

SPELT AND KAMUT

What Are They?
Spelt is a relative of wheat that has been popular in Europe for generations. It's now being incorporated into grain products sold in natural foods stores, and the flour is also available as whole spelt flour and white spelt flour.

Kamut (pronounced "kah-MOOT") is a type of wheat

that has its roots in ancient Egypt. Like spelt, it's increasingly being incorporated into grain products, such as breakfast cereals, sold in natural foods stores.

How Can I Use Them?

Use spelt and kamut the same way that you would use regular wheat flour, with one caveat: like amaranth, spelt and kamut cannot be the primary flours used if you are making yeast breads—the gluten quality is low. If you use spelt or kamut in yeast breads, mix them with wheat or another flour. You may need to experiment with different proportions in different recipes. A good place to start is one part spelt or kamut flour to three parts regular wheat flour.

• KAMUT WITH VEGETABLES •

2 teaspoons olive oil
1 cup chopped onions
2 teaspoons minced garlic
1½ cups vegetable broth
1 cup sliced carrots
1 cup sliced celery
1 bay leaf
1½ cups cooked small white beans, navy beans, or white kidney beans
½ cup sliced zucchini
½ cup sliced yellow squash
1 cup cooked kamut
¼ cup chopped fresh parsley

1. In a 3-quart saucepan, heat the oil over medium-high heat. Add the onions and garlic; cook, stirring, until softened, about 2 minutes.

2. Add the broth; bring to a boil. Add the carrots, celery, and bay leaf. Return to a boil; reduce the heat and simmer, uncovered, 20 minutes. Discard the bay leaf.
3. Add the beans, zucchini, yellow squash, kamut, and parsley. Simmer, uncovered, 10 minutes or until vegetables are tender and beans are heated through.

Makes 4 cups.

Nutrient content per ½ cup serving: Calories (Kcal): 96, Protein (gm): 4.5, Total fat (gm): 2, Saturated fat (gm): 0, Cholesterol (mg): 0, Dietary fiber (gm): 3, Sodium (mg): 29.5, Calcium (mg): 49, Iron (mg): 2, Zinc (mg): 1

TEFF

What Is It?

Teff is one of the oldest cultivated grains. It originated in Ethiopia, where is it used today to make the spongy, flat, round injera bread familiar to you if you have eaten in Ethiopian restaurants. Teff is a tiny grain that may be white, brown, or red in color.

....

Test Your Food Label Know-How

Let's say that you are shopping for a loaf of bread. When the label reads "wheat flour," what does this mean?

a) It means that the bread is made from white flour
b) It means that the bread is made from whole wheat flour

The answer is a. Wheat flour is white, refined flour, not the *whole* wheat flour that some people think it is. In other words, white equals wheat, but wheat does not equal whole wheat.

When you buy a bread or grain product, look for the word *whole* before the grains listed, as in *whole rye* and *whole oats*. Buy whole grain products as often as possible. If the entire product is not made from whole grains, buy a product in which at least the first ingredient listed is a whole grain. Ingredients are listed in order of their predominance in a product. Therefore, if a whole grain is listed first, at least 50 percent of that product is probably a whole grain.

How Can I Use It?

Teff can be used as a whole grain and cooked as a hot cereal *(see cooking instructions on page 47)*, or the flour can be used to make breads, muffins, and pancakes. As with amaranth and spelt, if you are making a yeast-raised bread, use part wheat flour and part teff flour. Starting with one part teff to three or four parts wheat flour is a good idea to ensure that the bread rises properly.

• HEARTY TEFF PANCAKES •

Cooked teff has a gelantinous texture and is very versatile. It can be added to puddings, pie fillings, baked goods, stews, and casseroles.

1 cup cooked teff
1 cup whole grain pancake mix
1 cup plain or vanilla fortified soy milk
2 egg whites, beaten (or equivalent commercial vegetarian egg replacer)
1 tablespoon vegetable oil

1. Preheat oiled skillet.
2. Stir ingredients together with a fork until thoroughly moistened.

3. Spoon batter onto skillet and cook over low to medium heat until golden brown.
4. Turn pancakes and cook on other side for about one minute or until edges are golden.
5. Sprinkle with powdered sugar and serve with warm maple syrup.

Serves 4.

Nutrient content per serving: Calories (Kcal): 252, Protein (gm): 11, Total fat (gm): 6, Saturated fat (gm): 1, Cholesterol (mg): 0, Dietary fiber (gm): 5, Sodium (mg): 586, Calcium (mg): 241, Iron (mg): 4, Zinc (mg): 0.11

Bulgur wheat is rolled, dried, cracked wheat. In the Middle East, it's used much the same way that rice is used in the West. Tabouli, a Middle-Eastern cold salad, is made with bulgur wheat. Bulgur wheat has a nutty flavor and can be used by itself as a side dish or hot cereal or in numerous ways in recipes such as casseroles, stuffing, and pilaf. Toss a handful into tomato-based pasta sauces or chili to thicken them and add a meaty texture.

NUTRITIONAL FEATURES

All five of the grains profiled here are good sources of protein, fiber, B vitamins, and minerals. Amaranth is particularly high in protein and the amino acids lysine and methionine. These grains are most often sold in natural foods stores in their unrefined states, so they retain all of their nutritive qualities, unlike the processed grains and flours that are sold in regular supermarkets.

Since grains take a relatively long time to cook, it's a good idea to make more than you need for that particular meal. Store the leftover grain in an airtight container in the refrigerator for up to a week. Leftovers can be reheated in a microwave oven or nonstick pan and eaten with another meal, or they can be added to other dishes such as soups, stews, casseroles—even pudding or hot cereal.

Buying and Storing Grains

Grains and grain flours can be purchased packaged or in bulk. Either way, they should be stored in a cool, dry place in an airtight container. Storing them in the refrigerator or freezer is better yet—it will keep the grains from going rancid as quickly and keep them fresh longer.

In India, dried beans such as garbanzo beans (also called chickpeas) are often ground and used as flour in bread making.

AISLE 2

LOBSTER

SEAFOOD

MEAT/POULTRY

MEAT ALTERNATIVES

TODAY'S FEATURES: FREE-RANGE AND ORGANIC MEATS, MEAT ALTERNATIVES

FREE-RANGE AND ORGANIC MEATS

What Are They?

The term *free-range* refers to meat and eggs from chickens that have been allowed to move freely around their habitat, as opposed to being confined in pens or cages. This is considered by many to be a more humane way to treat the birds than that practiced on factory farms. Humane treatment of animals raised for food products is a value that the natural foods industry generally respects and promotes.

Organic meat is the flesh of animals that have been raised without the use of hormones and antibiotics. Environmental contaminants and other residues accumulate in the greatest concentrations in animal fat and tissues. So, if you eat animal products, buying organic helps to minimize your exposure to these substances.

Nutritional Features

Free-range and organic meats are essentially the same, nutritionally, as their supermarket counterparts. The advantage to free-range and organic meats is their comparatively low levels of drug and hormone residues. All meats, however, are devoid of dietary fiber and beneficial phytochemicals, and all meats contribute cholesterol and saturated fat, substances that most of us consume in excess and that are associated with increased rates of coronary artery disease, cancer, obesity, and other diseases and conditions. Meats are good sources of protein and certain minerals, although these nutrients are also available in foods of plant origin.

How Can I Use Them?

Most of us were raised in a "meat and potatoes" tradition. Just ask any of your friends what they are planning for dinner tonight, and the answer will be a clue to their mindset about what constitutes a meal. If the answer is, "Chicken," "Fish," or "We're grilling out steak tonight," then it's obvious that, for them, meat is the focal point of the meal—the food around which the menu is planned. For most Westerners, meat is the foundation of the diet. Rice, potatoes, salad, other vegetables, fruit, and bread are comparatively unimportant "side dishes," or they aren't a part of the meal at all.

A more healthful approach to including meat in the diet is to use it sparingly. This way, you lessen your intake of saturated fat and cholesterol, you curb your protein intake (most of us get far too much), and you are likely to eat more fiber and nutrient-rich plant products.

Instead of eating large portions of meat as an entrée, choose more meals that use meat as a minor ingredient or a condiment, as the following examples show. You can decrease the amount of meat you use in these dishes as time goes by. Eventually, you can even make them meatless if you care to.

- Stir-fries made with a variety of vegetables and small chunks of lean meat, chicken, or seafood, served with plenty of steamed rice

- Many-bean chili made with a small amount of lean ground meat

- Vegetable stew—a colorful combination of carrots, potatoes, assorted beans, tomatoes, and corn with small pieces of lean meat

- Pasta topped with sautéed vegetables and small pieces of seafood in a marinara sauce

- Hearty lentil soup or bean soup with small pieces of meat for flavor

- Leftover chili, stew—even thick soups—can also be served over a big helping of steamed rice, polenta, couscous, or other grains such as quinoa or a mixture of millet and teff

MEAT ALTERNATIVES

Straight-Talk with Berke Breathed, creator of *Bloom Country* and *Outland* comic strips, Seattle, Washington
(from an April 1994 interview in *Seattle* magazine)

What do you say to people who say, "But we're a carnivorous race"?

Our jaws, teeth, and stomach are better designed for broccoli than prime rib. Animal fats make us die early.

Fruits and vegetables extend our lives. Cholesterol clogs
our veins like dirt in marine diesel injectors (a pet metaphor
that's close to my heart). Grains mysteriously clear them.
Raise a vegetarian kid for ten years and then give him a
bite of steak. He'll spew it on the ceiling. The whole carnivorous thing looks suspicious. It could be an old Nixon plot.

*Do you surround yourself with munchies when you're cre-
ating your strips?*
   Only free-range pretzels.

What Are They?

They look like burgers and hot dogs. They taste like burgers
and hot dogs. But they're meatless, and they contain no cholesterol and little, if any, saturated fat. Many actually contain
some fiber. What are they?

They're any of a large and growing number of vegetable-
and/or grain-based meat substitute products, from burger
patties and hot dogs to sausage links and patties, bacon, and
ground meat. They come in a wide range of flavors, tex-
tures, sizes and shapes, and they taste great. They're convenient, and nutritionally they're far superior to their real
meat counterparts.

Burger Patties

Even your neighborhood supermarket carries these now,
although, if you didn't know where to find them, you might
be surprised to learn that they're usually stocked in the
frozen food section, near the waffles and pancakes and other
breakfast items. Natural food stores have been carrying
these for years and still have the best selection.

Meatless burger patties come in many varieties; you will
need to experiment with several before settling on one or

two favorites. Many people like the Yves, Gardenburger, and Boca Burger brands, but there are many other good ones. Some are made from chopped vegetables and grains, such as rice, and others are soy-based. Some are spicy; some are not. Some contain egg whites; others are free of all animal products. Some are made to resemble cooked ground meat burgers in flavor, color, and texture, and some would never be mistaken for "the real thing."

Meatless Hot Dogs

These bear an amazing resemblance to the real thing. Like burger patties, there are some variations in flavor, color, texture, and ingredients from one brand to the next, but there's generally less variation in these than in burger patties. Try several brands to find the one you like the best. Tofu Pups and Smart Dogs are two that many people find exceptionally good.

If you plan to bring veggie burger patties or meatless hot dogs to a cookout or picnic, take more than you need. People will be curious, and the products look and smell so good that you can count on them wanting to try one. Bring extras so that you'll have enough for yourself or your family as well as some for others to sample.

Burger Crumbles

This product is generally frozen and packaged in a box or plastic bag (similar to a bag of frozen vegetables). It's made primarily of soy, resembles crumbled ground beef, and can be used in all of the same ways. Natural foods stores also carry meat substitutes that simulate other types of meat, such as chicken and tuna. These are sometimes made from wheat but are usually made from soy. They're sold in blocks or big chunks that are used in recipes in the same way that meat is used.

A similar product is plain textured vegetable protein (TVP), a soy product. It's sold dry in granules or chunks. In cooking, TVP absorbs the liquid in the recipe (tomato sauce or vegetable broth, for example) and reconstitutes into a chewy food that resembles meat.

TVP is used in all of the same ways that ground meat is used. You can find TVP packaged in bags and boxes on the grocery shelves, and it's often sold in bulk bins as well. It's also commonly found in vegetarian boxed mixes, such as Fantastic Foods vegetarian chili mix and others.

Meatless Sausages and Cold Cuts

Usually soy-based, these look, taste, and smell like the real thing. The sausages come in link or patty form, and the cold cuts are packaged the same way that their real meat counterparts are packaged but without the nitrites, a distinct advantage. Yves makes several good products, but you'll want to sample other brands as well to find your favorites.

How Can I Use Them?

Meat substitutes such as those described can be very useful for anyone who is trying to reduce their meat consumption. I think of them as transition foods for people who are still learning new-meal planning skills and are trying to move toward a healthier, more plant-based diet. The burger patties and hot dogs work well for picnics, backyard cookouts, and to have on hand at home for a quick and convenient snack or meal for anyone who is pressed for time and wants something that takes less than five minutes in the microwave.

Use burger crumbles and TVP to make burrito and taco fillings, chili, spaghetti sauce, nachos, sloppy joe filling, as pizza topping, and to add to casseroles. Use meatless hot dogs to make chili dogs or beans and franks.

• SLOPPY JOES •

(Reprinted by permission from *The Peaceful Palate* by
Jennifer Raymond)

1½ cups water
1 large onion, finely chopped
1 bell pepper, finely diced
1 cup textured vegetable protein
1 15-ounce can tomato sauce
1 tablespoon sugar or other sweetener
1 teaspoon chili powder
1 teaspoon garlic powder or granules
2 tablespoons cider vinegar
1 tablespoon soy sauce
1 teaspoon stone ground or Dijon mustard
4 whole wheat burger buns

Heat ½ cup of the water in a large pot, then add the chopped onion and bell pepper. Cook until the onion is soft, about 5 minutes. Add the remaining 1 cup of water, the textured vegetable protein, tomato sauce, sugar, chili powder, garlic powder, cider vinegar, soy sauce, and mustard. Cook over medium heat, stirring frequently, for 10 minutes.

Split the buns and warm them in a toaster oven. Top with a serving of sauce.

Makes 4 servings.

Nutrient content per serving: Calories (Kcal): 158, Protein (gm): 14, Total fat (gm): 1, Saturated fat (gm): 0, Cholesterol (mg): 0 Sodium (mg): 230

Nutritional Features

If you've gotta have a burger, or a hot dog, or a bologna sandwich, or a sausage biscuit for breakfast, then you're a whole lot better off eating one of these meat substitute products than their real meat counterparts.

For starters, these products are all cholesterol-free. Most are very low in saturated fat, and most are far lower in total fat than the "real thing." Some are fat-free. Not only do these products *not* contain what you *don't* want, but they often contribute what you do want. Some contain several grams of dietary fiber. In the case of products made from soy protein isolates, they may also contain substantial amounts of the health-promoting phytochemicals found in soy and other plant materials. Also, meatless hot dogs, sausage, and cold cuts generally contain less sodium than their meat counterparts, and they are free of the nitrates and nitrites often found in processed meats.

Take a look at how some common meat substitutes compare with their real meat counterparts:

Nutritional Comparisons of Selected Meatless Products and Their Meat Counterparts

(Sources: *Food Values of Portions Commonly Used* by Pennington and Church, or manufacturer)

	Hamburger (3.5 oz. cooked)	Veggie Burger (Boca Burger, Vegan Original, 1 patty)
Calories (Kcal):	289	84
Protein (gm):	24	12
Dietary Fiber (gm):	0	5
Total Fat (gm):	21	0
Saturated Fat (gm):	8	0

Cholesterol (mg):	90	0
Sodium (mg):	292	227

	Hot Dog (1 link)	**Vegetarian Hot Dog (Lightlife Tofu Pup, 1 link)**
Calories (Kcal):	180	60
Protein (gm):	7	8
Dietary Fiber (gm):	0	0
Total Fat (gm):	16	2.5
Saturated Fat (gm):	7	1
Cholesterol (mg):	35	0
Sodium (mg):	585	140

	Bacon, 3 strips broiled	**Vegetarian Bacon (Lightlife Fakin' Bacon, 3 strips)**
Calories (Kcal):	109	80
Protein (gm):	6	8
Dietary Fiber (gm):	0	1
Total Fat (gm):	9	2.5
Saturated Fat (gm):	3	0.5
Cholesterol (mg):	16	0
Sodium (mg):	303	230

	Sausage, one link	**Vegetarian Sausage (Soy Boy Leaner Wieners, one link)**
Calories (Kcal):	48	55
Protein (gm):	3	12
Dietary Fiber (gm):	0	0.5
Total Fat (gm):	4	0
Saturated Fat (gm):	1	0
Cholesterol (mg):	11	0
Sodium (mg):	168	140

AISLE 3

WINE	DRESSINGS
ORGANIC NONALCOHOLIC	OILS
PICKLES	VINEGAR

TODAY'S FEATURES: DRESSINGS, OIL, AND VINEGAR

BOTTLED SALAD DRESSINGS

What Are They (Why Are They Special?)

If you use commercial salad dressings, you may be getting tired of the usual lineup: French, Bleu cheese, Italian, and Thousand Island. If you've run the gamut of the fat-free varieties, you're probably even more tired of them. From my own experience sampling these dressings, and judging from the feedback I've gotten from my clients, there are one or two that taste pretty good; the others have a funky aftertaste and leave much to be desired.

Natural-food-brand bottled salad dressings are generally a better choice than those you'll find in a regular supermarket. For one thing, they contain about half the sodium (or less) than their mainstream counterparts. Their ingredients are pure and simple. You won't find artificial flavors and colors and other synthetic ingredients. And they come in a range of interesting flavors. How do Lemon Tahini Vinaigrette, Mango Mama, and

Lime Cilantro grab you? If you've never tried them, it's worth sampling a few types of natural salad dressings.

How Can I Use Them?

Besides using them on mixed green and other vegetable salads, use bottled salad dressings as a dip for fresh vegetable pieces, or as a spread on sandwiches. For instance, creamy dressings are good on grilled veggie Reuben sandwiches, and thick mustard dressings are good on toasted tomato sandwiches. Certain dressings go well with fresh fruit or fruit salads, too. For example, you can drizzle poppyseed dressing over fresh strawberries, or use a fruit-flavored dressing, such as mango, papaya, lemon, or lime. If you prefer not to make your own dressings from scratch, natural salad dressings can be a convenient condiment to have on hand.

• TANGERINE ZIP •

Some of the best salad dressings are the simplest. Remember your grandmother's vinegar-and-oil salads? They always tasted great. Even plain, blenderized fresh fruit can be light and refreshing over a plate of greens. Acidic fruits work well because they add a "zip" that can often take the place of salt. Try this one:

1 fresh tangerine (use an orange if tangerines are unavailable)
1 tablespoon fresh lemon juice (the juice from 1 or 2 wedges of a fresh lemon)

Peel the tangerine and remove the seeds. Break into sections and place sections into a food processor. Add lemon juice and blend until smooth. Serve over fresh mixed baby greens.

Serves 1.

Nutritional content: Calories (Kcal): 37, Protein (gm): 0.5, Total fat (gm): 0, Saturated fat (gm): 0, Cholesterol (mg): 0, Dietary fiber (gm): N/A, Sodium (mg): 1, Calcium (mg): 12, Iron (mg): 0.1, Zinc (mg): N/A

Nutritional Features

Natural bottled salad dressings are generally superior to the typical commercial types because they contain less sodium—about half as much as most regular dressings—they are often made with organically grown ingredients, and they contain no artificial colors, flavors, or other synthetic ingredients.

Comparison of Sodium Contents of Natural and Regular Salad Dressings

(Sources: Manufacturer and *Food Values of Portions Commonly Used* by Pennington and Church)

Natural Food Brand Dressings	Serving Size	Sodium (mg)
Ayla's Lemon Mustard Salad Dressing	2 Tbsp.	140
Annie's Gingerly Vinaigrette	2 Tbsp.	190
Nasoya Vegi-Dressing Garden Herb	2 Tbsp.	135
Rising Sun Farm Oil-Free Pesto Sun-Dried Tomato	2 Tbsp.	70
Regular Brand Dressings		
Kraft Catalina	2 Tbsp.	370
Italian	2 Tbsp.	232
Russian	2 Tbsp.	266
Low-Calorie Thousand Island	2 Tbsp.	306

Storing Salad Dressings

Once you open the bottle, salad dressing needs refrigeration. Most will keep in the refrigerator for several months, including homemade varieties made with vinegar, oil, and spices. Homemade dressings made with fresh fruits and juices will keep for about one week in the refrigerator.

OIL

What Is It? (Why Is It Special?)

Every food store carries bottled vegetable oils. For all-purpose cooking and baking, corn oil, safflower oil, canola oil, and olive oil are the best choices. Vegetable oils carried in natural foods stores have not been chemically treated. Many are cold-pressed, which means that they have been processed with less friction and heat than commercial oils and have a higher nutrient content (especially those that are the product of the first pressing).

Personally, I add very little oil, if any, to the foods that I prepare. I keep small bottles of extra-virgin olive oil and corn oil on hand for general cooking purposes, and I use them sparingly. Beyond the most common types of oil, though, I also like to shop for specialty oils at the natural foods store. In my refrigerator, for instance, I have small bottles of walnut oil, lime-flavored oil, and orange oil.

Oils can be flavored with fruit essences, and they can also be infused with flavors from herbs and spices. Just a few drops of one of these oils can add a lot of flavor to foods. There are dozens of flavored or infused oils, including tarragon, garlic, porcini mushroom, apricot, sesame, grapefruit, hot pepper, and many, many more.

How Can I Use Them?

I like to vary the personality of some of my favorite recipes by occasionally adding a highly flavored oil. For instance, I sometimes add a teaspoon of walnut oil to my homemade vinaigrette dressing—it adds a wonderful, unique flavor to a mixed green salad. Another example: a teaspoon of hot pepper oil added to cooked pasta, salad dressing, or stir-fried vegetables adds loads of flavor for a relatively small amount of extra fat. If I'm going to steam kale in a skillet, I might add a teaspoon of seasoned oil—sesame, for instance—to the bottom of the pan. It keeps the minced garlic that I usually add from sticking to the bottom of the pan, and it adds flavor, too.

• SPICY HOMEMADE VINAIGRETTE DRESSING •

This is one of my all-time favorite homemade salad dressings. It's good on cold vegetable salads as well as on mixed greens.

1 teaspoon lemon juice (I use the juice of 1 or 2 fresh lemon wedges)
1 tablespoon red wine vinegar
2 tablespoons extra-virgin olive oil
2 teaspoons of your favorite salsa
1/4 teaspoon paprika
A sprinkling of freshly minced tarragon leaves (or 1/8 teaspoon dried tarragon leaves)
Salt, if desired (I usually leave it out)

Combine all ingredients in a small pitcher and mix well. Chill. Whisk together once more just before serving. This dressing works well on marinated vegetable salads.

Yield: 2 servings.

Nutritional content per serving: Calories (Kcal): 123, Protein (gm): 0.1, Total fat (gm): 13.5, Saturated fat (gm): 2, Cholesterol (mg): 0, Dietary fiber (gm): 0, Sodium (mg): 18, Calcium (mg): 1, Iron (mg): 0.1, Zinc (mg): 0

Nutritional Features

If you add fat to your food, the best choices for health are olive oil and canola oil. These are monounsaturated fats. Unlike saturated fats (such as butter and other animal fats) and trans fats (hydrogenated fats, including margarine), monounsaturated fats do not increase your risk of coronary artery disease.

Extra-virgin olive oil comes from the first pressing of the olives. It contains the most flavor and may contain more health-promoting phytochemicals than other types of olive oil, which come from further pressings of the olives. When a recipe calls for a more neutrally flavored fat, canola oil or even corn or safflower oil are acceptable choices. Flavored or infused oils are usually made with soybean oil or olive oil as the base, which is also fine.

In recipes for baked goods, the fat can usually be cut back by at least one third without adversely affecting the quality of the finished product. For instance, if a muffin recipe calls for one cup of oil, you can use ⅔ cup instead, and the muffins should come out just fine. You can also substitute pureed fruit (such as prunes or applesauce) for part or all of the oil in certain recipes. See Aisle 4: Fruit Puree Fat Substitutes for more information.

Buying and Storing Oil

Vegetable oils should be stored in a cool, dark place or in your refrigerator. This keeps them from oxidizing as quickly and prevents them from going rancid. To check the freshness of an oil, open the bottle and sniff. If the oil smells slightly fruity, it's fine. If it smells like turpentine, then it's gone rancid and should be thrown away.

I keep most of my oils in the refrigerator, but I keep my olive oil in the cupboard, since it turns cloudy or clumpy in the refrigerator. I also buy small bottles of oil, rather than the larger, economy sizes, since I don't use much. Though ounce for ounce, the larger bottles are usually less expensive, I find that by buying the small bottles, I use them up and replace them more often, thereby ensuring that what's on hand is fresh.

VINEGAR

What Is It? (Why Is It Special?)

If all you ever use is white vinegar or cider vinegar, then you're missing out on some terrific products. Like lemon juice, vinegar is acidic and adds a kick to whatever it's used in. Have you ever tried hot-and-sour soup at a Chinese restaurant? It's the vinegar that gives it its "punch." So, vinegar is a useful condiment to have on hand, because adding vinegar to foods can mean that you can reduce the amount of salt—and even fat—that you would otherwise add. And, like flavored oils, vinegar is available in many flavors and varieties.

My personal favorites include balsamic vinegar, plain and seasoned rice vinegar, raspberry vinegar, and malt vinegar. They're staples in my house.

Balsamic vinegar is made from wine grapes, and it's very rich and sweet. You'll probably use too much the first time you try it. A little bit goes a long way. Remember that when you see how much it costs. Just a teaspoon or two adds all the flavor you need to a green salad. Restaurants usually add oil and herbs to balsamic vinegar to make a balsamic vinaigrette dressing. At home, I usually use it straight. It tastes that good. Purists may tell you that balsamic vinegar is rightfully served with fresh fruit—over a bowl of strawberries, for example—but I love it on salad greens and potatoes.

Plain rice vinegar is very light and mildly sweet. It's great in marinated vegetable salads or confetti coleslaw. Seasoned rice vinegar has some sodium added, but it's delicious. The red pepper variety is addictive. Malt vinegar is delicious with potatoes. Also sample some of the fruit- and herb-flavored vinegars—raspberry, mango, papaya, tarragon, garlic, dill—the list goes on!

• CONFETTI COLESLAW •

This recipe takes only a few minutes to make using a food processor. Feel free to add green onions or other shredded fresh vegetables that you may have on hand such as yellow squash or zucchini. If you add additional vegetables, estimate or measure the amount you've added and add proportionately more dressing.

3 cups shredded cabbage
1/2 cup shredded carrot
1/2 cup chopped green pepper
1/3 cup rice vinegar (optional: use seasoned rice vinegar with
*   red pepper [note that using seasoned rice vinegar adds*
*   213 mg sodium to each serving of coleslaw])*
2 tablespoons vegetable oil (corn, safflower, or canola)

Place cabbage, carrot, and green pepper in a mixing bowl and toss gently. In a separate small bowl or cup, combine the rice vinegar and oil and whisk together. Add this to the cabbage mixture and toss again.

Makes 6 half-cup servings.

Nutritional content per serving: Calories (Kcal): 56, Protein (gm): 1, Total fat (gm): 5, Saturated fat (gm): 1, Cholesterol (mg): 0, Dietary fiber (gm): 1, Sodium (mg): 14, Iron (mg): 0.5, Calcium (mg): 16, Zinc(mg): 0

How Can I Use It?

Sure, you can use vinegar alone or mixed with oil as a salad dressing. But there are some other creative ways to use it as well. Try adding a little fruit juice to cider vinegar to give it a different flavor. You can also whisk plain yogurt into vinegar to make a creamy dressing.

• EVERYONE'S FAVORITE HOME FRIES •

This is a no-measure, foolproof recipe that you'll make over and over again. Leftovers taste great reheated.

Several white potatoes
Vegetable oil spray
Garlic powder
Oregano
Cayenne pepper
Paprika

1. Coat a baking sheet with vegetable oil spray or rub with a thin layer of olive oil. Preheat oven to 350 degrees F.
2. Wash several white potatoes and cut them into wedges. Dump them into a mixing bowl.
3. Sprinkle the potato wedges with several liberal shakes of garlic powder, oregano, cayenne pepper, and paprika. The cayenne pepper will make these hot and spicy, so vary the amount you use according to your "heat" tolerance. Toss wedges until coated.

4. Spread the wedges on the baking sheet and spray them with a thin layer of vegetable oil.
5. Bake for 30 or 40 minutes or until the potatoes are soft.
6. Serve with malt vinegar for dipping.

Yield varies depending upon how many potatoes you've used.

Nutritional content per 1 cup serving: Calories (Kcal): 220, Protein (gm): 5, Total fat (gm): 0.5, Saturated fat (gm): 0, Cholesterol (mg): 0, Dietary fiber (gm): 4, Sodium (mg): 16, Iron (mg): 3, Calcium (mg): 20, Zinc (mg): 1

Nutritional Features
Vinegar contains only traces of nutrients. Seasoned rice vinegar contains a fair amount of sodium (240 mg of sodium per tablespoon in the red pepper variety).

Storing Vinegar
Once opened, vinegar should be kept in the refrigerator.

AISLE 4

SPICES

BAKING

NUT BUTTERS

JAMS

PASTA

SAUCES

MAYONNAISE

CONDIMENTS

TODAY'S FEATURES: VEGETARIAN EGG REPLACER, NUT BUTTERS, SOY MAYONNAISE, WHOLE GRAIN BAKING MIXES, ORGANIC CANNED TOMATOES

VEGETARIAN EGG REPLACER

What Is It?

There are a variety of egg substitutes on the market, including powdered egg whites and the frozen, liquid egg substitutes that are made by mainstream companies using egg whites and yellow food coloring. These aren't for everyone. Personally, I'd prefer to avoid synthetic food coloring. Many people prefer to avoid animal products, including eggs and egg whites. Furthermore, frozen egg substitutes can be inconvenient. How many times have you used part of a container, only to store the remainder in the refrigerator and have to throw it away a few days later before it spoils?

I've found a much better solution. It's a powdered egg substitute called Egg Replacer made by Ener-G Foods. It actually contains no egg at all, but it works wonderfully in virtually any recipe—sweet or savory—that calls for eggs.

Egg Replacer is a blend of potato starch, tapioca flour, leavening agents (calcium lactate, calcium carbonate, and citric acid), and carbohydrate gum. The calcium lactate is not derived from dairy and does not contain lactose, so this is a product that strict vegetarians, or vegans, can use. The ingredients are all natural.

How Can I Use It?

Egg Replacer can be used in place of eggs in almost any recipe that calls for eggs. It can be used to make cookies, cakes, breads, muffins, custard, pudding, mousse, quiche, mayonnaise, and the list goes on. It works particularly well in baked goods and does not change the texture of the finished product as compared to similar products made with eggs. About the only types of foods that might not be candidates for this product would be those that are essentially cooked eggs, such as fried eggs, omelettes, or egg salad. For that purpose, you would be better off using tofu as an egg substitute *(see Aisle 7)*.

Egg Replacer is generally used in a ratio of 1½ teaspoons of Egg Replacer mixed with 2 tablespoons of water. This replaces one egg in recipes. If the recipe calls for two eggs, use twice as much Egg Replacer and water. When a recipe calls for egg whites beaten stiff, then the Egg Replacer can be beaten with the water until stiff. I've found Egg Replacer to work well in every recipe I've tried.

• MY FAVORITE CAROB CHIP COOKIES •

Egg Replacer works well in cookie recipes—just replace the eggs called for in traditional recipes with an equivalent amount of Egg Replacer. In this recipe, the Egg Replacer substitutes for two whole eggs.

1 tablespoon Egg Replacer
4 tablespoons water
2¼ cups unsifted all-purpose flour
1 teaspoon baking soda
1 teaspoon salt
1 cup organic butter, softened (or substitute ⅔ cup vegetable oil)
¾ cup sugar
¾ cup firmly packed brown sugar
1 teaspoon pure vanilla extract
12 ounces carob chips

1. Preheat the oven to 375 degrees F.
2. In a small dish or cup, whisk together the Egg Replacer and water. Set aside.
3. In another bowl, combine flour, baking soda, and salt. Set aside.
4. In a large mixing bowl, cream together the butter, sugar, brown sugar, and vanilla. Add the Egg Replacer mixture and beat well.
5. Gradually add the flour mixture, mixing well after each addition.
6. Fold in the carob chips.
7. Drop by rounded teaspoons onto ungreased cookie sheets.
8. Bake at 375 degrees F for 8–10 minutes or until lightly browned. Do not overcook.

Yield: About 7½ dozen (90 cookies).

Nutritional content per cookie: Calories (Kcal): 62, Protein (gm): 0.5, Total fat (gm): 3, Saturated fat (gm): 2, Cholesterol (mg): 5, Dietary fiber (gm): 0, Sodium (mg): 54, Iron (mg): 0.3, Calcium (mg): 4, Zinc (mg): 0

Nutritional Features

Egg Replacer is free of cholesterol, fat, and sodium. It contains only ten calories in one teaspoon. It actually contains only trace amounts of vitamins and minerals, although one teaspoonful does provide forty milligrams of calcium.

Buying and Storing Egg Replacer

Egg Replacer is generally sold in a one-pound box. Depending upon how often you use it, a box can last several months to a year or longer. It's economical. Once I open the box, I store it in an airtight plastic bag in the cupboard or refrigerator just like I store my open boxes of baking soda and baking powder, to help it stay fresh and to catch any spillage.

....

Homemade Egg Substitutes

In recipes for baked goods that yield a relatively large batch, such as a cookie recipe that yields dozens of cookies, or a loaf of quick bread, the eggs can often just be left out without making a big difference in the texture of the product. This is especially true when the recipe calls for only one or two eggs. In that case, you can often just add a little bit of liquid—a tablespoon or two of water, juice, milk, or soy milk—for each egg, just to maintain the intended moisture level of the product.

In baked good recipes that call for more than two eggs, the following can be used to replace each egg:

- ¼ cup tofu blended with the liquid ingredients in the recipe
- ½ ripe, mashed banana
- 2 tablespoons of cornstarch

- 1 tablespoon of flour blended with 2 tablespoons of water
- 1 tablespoon of flaxseeds blended with ¼ cup of water
- ¼ cup of applesauce, canned pumpkin, or canned squash

Eggs are included in baked goods recipes more for their effect on texture than for their binding quality. In recipes that require a binder, you can try substituting mashed potatoes, cooked oatmeal, tomato paste, finely crushed bread crumbs, or a combination of these foods, for eggs. The amounts used will vary from recipe to recipe, but a good starting point is about a quarter cup of any of these ingredients or a mixture to replace one egg.

NUT BUTTERS

What Are They?

Nut butters are any type of nut that has been blended into a creamy paste. Most of us were raised on peanut butter sandwiches. You aren't as likely to have tried cashew butter or almond butter, but they're nutritious and can be a nice change of pace. Tahini, or blenderized sesame seeds, is another type of butter that is versatile, delicious, and packed with vitamins and minerals.

In regular supermarkets, commercial brands of peanut butter typically contain sugar, salt, and hydrogenated fats. The added hydrogenated fats help to keep the oil from the peanuts from separating and rising to the surface. Natural peanut butter and other natural nut butters may or may not have added salt, but they generally don't have added sugar and they never contain hydrogenated fat. That's why you'll see a layer of oil floating at the top of the jar when you buy natural nut butters. Just stir it in before using.

Some people like to store jars of natural nut butter upside down in the cupboard. This keeps the oil from settling on top of the jar. Instead, it goes to the bottom. When you flip the jar over to use the nut butter, you don't have the inconvenience of having to stir the oil back in. If you try this trick, be sure that the lid is screwed on tightly. Even so, I've found that I sometimes get a little leakage onto the shelf. You might want to keep a plate or a piece of paper toweling under the jar, just in case.

One more note: it might have occurred to you that you could just pour off the oil at the top of the jar to make the nut butter easier and neater to handle. If you do this, you'll need a pickax to get the nut butter out of the jar. A better method is to refrigerate the nut butter after you've stirred in the oil to keep it from separating.

How Can I Use Them?

Nut butters are a classic sandwich filling, because they don't need refrigeration (they're perfect for brown-bag lunches, hikes in the mountains, and long road trips), and everyone likes the taste. A tablespoon of peanut butter adds lots of flavor to a vegetable stir-fry, and a couple tablespoons of tahini adds richness and lots of calcium to puréed chickpeas, or hummus. Here are a few more ways to use nut (and seed) butters. You'll find many more yourself:

- Put any kind of nut butter on celery sticks (stick some raisins on top for "ants-on-a-log," although I never found that name to be very appealing!).

- Spread nut butters on toasted English muffin halves, bagels, or whole-grain toast.

- Start with a thin layer of nut butter and add slices of apples, pears, or bananas to a sandwich.

- Blend nut butter with a little honey and/or chopped, dried fruit pieces for a sandwich filling or spread for toast or crackers.

- Blend nut butters into basic white sauce *(see recipe for Peanutty Sauce)* and serve over vegetables, lentil loaf (and other vegetarian versions of the all-American meat loaf), pilafs, vegetable and grain patties, and croquettes.

- Nut butters and tahini can be used in creamy salad dressings, as an ingredient in baked goods such as cookies and muffins, and in soups.

• PEANUTTY SAUCE •

In this recipe, peanut butter is blended into a basic white sauce to make a versatile sauce that can be spooned over steamed vegetables, veggie burger patties, vegetarian loaves, and other foods. It can also be used as a dip for vegetable sticks. The recipe calls for butter, which most chefs consider indispensable for a white sauce, but vegans can substitute corn oil if desired.

2 tablespoons organic butter (vegans use 2 tablespoons corn oil)
2 tablespoons white flour
1 cup vegetable broth, unsalted (milk or soymilk can also be used)
1 tablespoon creamy peanut butter

Over low heat, melt the butter in a small saucepan. Add the flour, blending well with a small whisk or a fork. Continue stirring for 3 to 4 minutes, being careful not to let the flour stick to the bottom of the pan or scorch. Slowly stir in the vegetable broth. Add the peanut butter and stir until well blended. Simmer and stir the sauce for several minutes until it is thickened and hot, but don't let it boil. Remove from heat and serve.

Makes about 1¼ cups.

Nutritional content per ¼ cup serving: Calories (Kcal): 70, Protein (gm): 1.5, Total fat (gm): 6, Saturated fat (gm): 3 (less or none if animal products are not used), Cholesterol (mg): 12 (none if animal products are not used), Dietary fiber (gm): 0, Sodium (mg): 47 (less if unsalted peanut butter is used), Iron (mg): 0.1, Calcium (mg): 2, Zinc (mg): 0

Nutritional Features

Nut and seed butters can be high in protein, dietary fiber, and a variety of vitamins and minerals. They're high in calories and fat, too, although the fat is unsaturated. It's generally wise to use nuts, seeds, and nut and seed butters sparingly—as you would a condiment—due to the calorie content. Aside from issues of weight control, though, there's no reason not to enjoy them in the ways described above.

Nutrients in 2 Tablespoons of Nut and Seed Butters
(Source: Manufacturer)

	Arrowhead Mills Peanut Butter	Arrowhead Mills Sesame Tahini
Calories (Kcal):	200	190
Protein (gm):	8	6
Total Fat (gm):	15	19
Saturated Fat (gm):	3	3

Cholesterol (gm):	0	0
Dietary Fiber (gm):	2	3
Sodium (mg):	100	5
Calcium (mg):	0	40

	Marantha Roasted Almond Butter	Marantha Roasted Cashew Butter
Calories (Kcal):	220	210
Protein (gm):	8	8
Total Fat (gm):	18	16
Saturated Fat (gm):	1	2
Cholesterol (gm):	0	0
Dietary Fiber (gm):	6	6
Sodium (mg):	0	9
Calcium (mg):	100	0

Buying and Storing Nut Butters

For the freshest-tasting nut butters, grind your own at home or at the store from whole nuts. A food processor or heavy-duty blender works best. For very small quantities, you can even use a coffee-bean grinder or a small (one cup) capacity mini–food processor.

Whether fresh or bottled, though, nut (and seed) butters don't need refrigeration. Just make sure that the container is sealed tightly, and they'll keep in your cupboard for several months. Some people do prefer to store them in the refrigerator, though, to keep them freshest. That's fine, but cold nut butter is harder to spread than at room temperature.

SOY "MAYONNAISE"

What Is It?

Legally, it can't actually be called "mayonnaise" because it doesn't fit the standard of identity for that product (like the difference between "cheese" and "cheese food," or "fruit juice" and "fruit drink"). So, it's called "vegi dressing and spread" or something similar, and it's used in all the same ways as traditional mayonnaise. The difference: soy mayonnaise is free of saturated fat and cholesterol, because it's made with tofu, canola oil, and other natural ingredients.

Regular mayonnaise is made with eggs, but soy mayonnaise is typically free of animal products, so strict vegetarians or vegans can usually use it. Examples of brands that contain no animal products are Nayonaise and Vegenaise. These products taste great, and they're just as versatile as regular mayonnaise. Hain brand makes Eggless Mayonnaise Dressing which, as the label notes, contains no eggs. It does contain dairy products, however.

How Can I Use It?

Use soy mayonnaise straight from the jar as a sandwich spread or as an ingredient in sandwich fillings *(see the recipe for Sunny Tofu Salad on page 85)*, dips, other spreads, and so on. You can use it any way that you would use regular mayonnaise, so substitute it cup for cup in any recipe that calls for mayonnaise. You'll find the flavor of soy "mayonnaise" to be similar to commercial salad dressings—sweeter and a bit lighter than real mayonnaise.

Nutritional Features

Soy mayonnaise is nutritionally superior to regular mayonnaise, because it's free of saturated fat and cholesterol. It's also substantially lower in total fat and calories.

Comparison of Nutrients in
One Tablespoon of Soy Mayonnaise and
One Tablespoon of Regular Mayonnaise
(Source: Manufacturer)

	Nasoya/Nayonaise Vegi Dressing & Spread	Best Foods/ Hellmann's Mayonnaise
Calories (Kcal):	35	100
Total fat (gm):	3	11
Saturated fat (gm):	0	1.7
Cholesterol (mg):	0	7
Sodium (mg):	105	80

Buying and Storing Soy Mayonnaise

After the jar is opened, store soy mayonnaise in the refrigerator.

• SUNNY TOFU SALAD •

This is an "all soy" recipe, using tofu and soy mayonnaise instead of animal products to make everyone's favorite sandwich filling. Use firm tofu to replace the egg in your favorite recipe for egg salad, and you'll be amazed at how closely it resembles the "real thing." Tofu has the consistency of cooked egg whites, so it really is ideal for this recipe (*read more about tofu in Aisle 7*).

8 ounces of water-packed tofu or one 10.5 ounce container
    of silken tofu (aseptically packaged)
1 tablespoon of yellow mustard
1/2 teaspoon of paprika
2 celery stalks, minced
1/4 cup pickle relish
1/4 teaspoon of black pepper

2 scallions, minced
1/2 cup soy mayonnaise

Mash the tofu with a fork. Stir in remaining ingredients. Chill. Use as a sandwich filling or for stuffed tomatoes.

Yield: About four 1/3 cup servings.

Nutrient content per serving: Calories (Kcal): 180, Protein (gm): 9, Total fat (gm): 11, Saturated fat (gm): 1.7, Cholesterol (mg): 0, Dietary fiber (gm): 1, Sodium (mg): 347, Calcium (mg): 131

WHOLE-GRAIN BAKING MIXES

What Are They?

They include mixes for pancakes, waffles, breads, brownies, cookies, gingerbread, and other baked goods, as well as all-purpose baking mixes. They're the same sorts of convenience products—quick mixes for all types of baked products—that people buy every day in supermarkets. The twist: whereas the kind you'll find in regular supermarkets are full of refined white flour, hydrogenated fats, artificial flavorings and colorings, sodium, and a host of other less-than-ideal ingredients, natural mixes consist mostly or entirely of organic, whole-grain flours. Ingredient lists tend to be short because they're free of hydrogenated fats, artificial flavorings and colorings, and synthetic preservatives.

How Can I Use Them?

You'll pay more for a batch of cookies made from a mix than for cookies made from scratch, but convenience is often worth the extra cost. Even fifteen minutes saved gathering and measuring ingredients makes baking mixes a worthwhile luxury for many people. Nice to know, though, that the convenience doesn't have to have a nutritional cost.

Many natural baking mixes are free of animal products, so they're cholesterol-free, too. And since they're free of hydrogenated fats, they usually contain little or no saturated fat. That is, of course, until you add the eggs called for in the instructions. Or the milk. Or the butter.

Many of these product packages provide instructions for omitting the eggs and fat. If the information isn't provided, make the substitutions on your own. Vegetarian egg replacer, mashed bananas, and tofu can replace eggs, or just leave the eggs out altogether and add a little extra liquid *(see page 78)*. Milk can be replaced with soy milk, butter with applesauce, mashed pumpkin, or a little vegetable oil.

Use natural baking mixes to save time and to make life a little easier for yourself.

Muffins, cookies, and quick breads freeze well. Why not be a Sunday cook this weekend and bake a batch or loaf or two? Store them in the freezer. You'll have something on hand to offer friends when they drop by. Individual muffins, cookies, and mini-loaves of bread can be taken out one at a time as needed for bag lunches or to cure a sweet tooth. When the week gets harried and you're too pooped to lift a finger, you'll be so glad to have a few homemade somethings in your freezer.

Nutritional Features

Whole-grain baking mixes can be the foundation of foods that are good sources of dietary fiber and a range of vitamins and minerals. The ingredients that *don't* come with the mix—eggs, milk, butter, and oil—or the substitutes for those ingredients, can add varying amounts of fat, saturated fat, and cholesterol. It's up to you how much or how little.

Here's how three mixes I recommend stack up before eggs, milk, fat, or substitutes for these ingredients are added.

UpCountry Naturals Multigrain Organic Pancake Mix
Ingredients: Whole-grain wheat flour, whole rye flour, whole cornmeal flour, whole buckwheat flour, buttermilk powder, nonaluminum baking powder, salt.

Nutrients per ¼ cup of mix: Calories (Kcal): 110, Protein (gm): 4, Total fat (gm): 0.5, Saturated fat (gm): 0, Cholesterol (mg): 0, Dietary fiber (gm): 3, Sodium (gm): 330, Calcium (mg): 100, Iron (mg): 1

Arrowhead Mills Brownie Mix
Ingredients: Unbleached cane sugar, whole-grain white wheat flour, nonalkalized natural cocoa powder, dried egg whites, natural vanilla powder, sea salt, baking soda, and lecithin.

Nutrients per serving (1 brownie): Calories (Kcal): 110, Protein (gm): 2, Total fat (gm): 0, Saturated fat (gm): 0, Cholesterol (mg): 0, Dietary fiber (gm): 2, Sodium (mg): 100, Calcium (mg): 40, Iron (mg): 0.4

Old Savannah Organic Gingerbread Cake & Cookie Mix
Ingredients: Whole-wheat pastry flour, evaporated sugar-cane juice, whole-wheat-bread flour, spices, roasted carob powder, baking soda, salt, soy flour.

Nutrients per ¼ cup of mix: Calories (Kcal): 140, Protein (gm): 4, Total fat (gm): 0.5, Saturated fat (gm): 0, Cholesterol (mg): 0, Dietary fiber (gm): 3, Sodium (mg): 300, Calcium (mg): 200, Iron (mg): 1.8

Buying and Storing Baking Mixes

Baking mixes are sometimes available in the bulk section of the natural foods store. If you buy in bulk, store the mix in an airtight container in your cupboard for up to a month or in your refrigerator or freezer. Likewise, when you buy boxed mixes, store any unused portion in your cupboard or refrigerator. Since the boxes never close tightly after they've been opened, I always seal the whole opened box in a Ziploc-style plastic bag in my cupboard. This helps keep the mix fresh but also keeps out pests—an important sanitation precaution, particularly in warm climates where insects more commonly find their way into homes. Alternately, store opened boxes of mix in your refrigerator.

If you keep any natural flour or grain product for more than a month, you should store it in the refrigerator or freezer. This will prevent them from becoming infested with grain moths. Unfortunately, sealed packages and airtight containers aren't sufficient protection from these pests.

• HEALTHY PANCAKES •

You can make your own pancake and waffle mix by combining the dry ingredients in this recipe and storing them in an airtight container. When you are ready to use it, just add the liquid ingredients.

These pancakes are a tradition in my family. Late-sleepers will leap out of bed on Saturday morning when they smell "Healthies" on the griddle.

1 cup whole wheat flour
½ cup white or soy flour
⅓ cup wheat germ
1 teaspoon baking soda

1 teaspoon cinnamon
1 tablespoon baking powder
½ teaspoon salt
1¾ cups fortified soy milk
¼ cup vegetable oil
Vegetarian Egg Replacer equivalent to one egg
2 egg whites, beaten (or substitute equivalent amount of Vegetarian Egg Replacer, beaten stiff)

Note: omit salt to lower sodium content of recipe. I recommend leaving in the vegetable oil, rather than substituting applesauce or other fruit puree, because the batter is very heavy.

Stir the soy milk, vegetable oil, and Egg Replacer into the dry ingredients. Fold in the beaten egg whites. Ladle onto a hot griddle.

Yield: About 6 large pancakes.

Nutrient content per pancake: Calories (Kcal): 262, Protein (gm): 8.5, Total fat (gm): 11, Saturated fat (gm): 1, Cholesterol (mg): 0, Dietary fiber (gm): 3.5, Sodium (mg): 530, Calcium (mg): 95, Iron (mg): 2, Zinc (mg): 2

ORGANIC CANNED TOMATOES

What Are They? (Why Are They Special?)

Well, they're just canned tomatoes—stewed, diced, whole with basil, sauce, paste—that staple of every cupboard. But that's just it—they're used so often, in so many recipes. Tomatoes are one of the crops that suffer from heavy use of pesticides. Commercial canned varieties also tend to be very high in sodium. That's why I like to buy the organic tomato products that I find in my natural foods store. They've been grown without the use of synthetic pesticides, and they're usually lower in sodium than the commercial brands. There's a wide enough range available to suit my every need, whether it's a stew, soup, pasta sauce, pizza topping, or casserole.

They also happen to taste better. I thought that might be my imagination, until I learned that at least one well-known brand of canned organic tomatoes (Muir Glen) was found in an independent study to taste better than regular supermarket brands. You can judge for yourself.

How Can I Use Them?
Use organic canned tomato products to make everything from soups, stews, sauces, casseroles—you name it.

• SIMPLE BLACK BEAN STEW •

My meals tend to be prepared simply. Here's an example of how I use canned tomatoes to fix a quick supper.

1 tablespoon olive oil
Small yellow onion, chopped
1 teaspoon minced garlic
15-ounce can of crushed tomatoes
15-ounce can of black beans, rinsed and drained
1/2 cup diced green pepper
1/2 cup frozen corn kernels
1/2 teaspoon freshly ground black pepper

Pour olive oil into a large skillet. Tip the pan to distribute the oil. Add the garlic and chopped onion and cook over medium heat until onion is translucent. Add tomatoes, beans, green pepper, corn, and black pepper. Mix well, then cover pan and let simmer, stirring occasionally, for about 30 minutes. Serve over steamed rice or another cooked grain.

Makes about 5 cups.

Nutritional content per cup: Calories (Kcal): 149, Protein (gm): 8, Total fat (gm): 3, Saturated fat (gm): 0.5, Cholesterol (mg): 0, Dietary fiber (gm): 4, Sodium (mg): 158, Iron (mg): 2, Calcium (mg): 45, Zinc (mg): 1.0

Bottled spaghetti sauces can be rich due to added sweeteners and vegetable oil. This is especially true of commercial brands sold in regular supermarkets. To dilute a too-rich or too-sweet flavor in these ready-to-use sauces, add a few scoops of the sauce to a can of organic tomato sauce or organic crushed or stewed tomatoes. Dump a can of organic tomatoes into a mixing bowl, then add the bottled sauce one scoop at a time, stirring and tasting after each addition until the mixture tastes right to you.

Nutritional Features

Organic canned tomato products are a good source of vitamins A and C, and they provide some iron, too. They're relatively high in sodium, but they're lower in sodium than mainstream brands. Some products are available with no salt added.

Nutrients in ½ Cup of Canned Tomato Product
(Source: Manufacturer)

	Eden Crushed Tomatoes
Calories (Kcal):	40
Protein (gm):	2
Total fat (gm):	0
Saturated fat (gm):	0
Cholesterol (mg):	0
Dietary fiber (gm):	2
Sodium (mg):	0
Vitamin A (I.U.):	1,500
Vitamin C (mg):	18
Iron (mg):	1.4

	Italian Style Diced	Muir Glen Stewed	Whole Peeled with Basil
Calories (Kcal):	25	25	30
Protein (gm):	1	1	1
Total fat (gm):	0	0	0
Saturated fat (gm):	0	0	0
Cholesterol (mg):	0	0	0
Dietary fiber (gm):	1	1	1
Sodium (mg):	290	190	260
Vitamin A (I.U.):	500	500	750
Vitamin C (mg):	12	12	12
Iron (mg):	1	1	1

Buying and Storing Organic Canned Tomatoes
Whatever you don't use after you've opened the can should be stored in another covered container (not in the can) in the refrigerator and used within a week or two.

AISLE 5

JUICE	PET
SODA POP	CLEANING
SPRITZERS	SOY MILK

TODAY'S FEATURES: SOY MILK, RICE MILK, AND OTHER MILK SUBSTITUTES

SOY MILK

What Is It?

Soy milk is a creamy milk made from whole soybeans that have been ground, cooked, and soaked. The milk is then pressed out of the beans. Soy milk has a mild, "beanie" flavor that many people find quite appealing. In addition to plain, soy milk is also sold in other flavors, including chocolate (or carob), vanilla, and strawberry. Many brands are available in a "lite" or reduced-fat variety, and many are also fortified with extra vitamins and minerals.

You won't see the word *soy milk* on package labels, even though it's commonly referred to as such by shoppers and nutritionists. Just as soy "mayonnaise" has to be labeled as something other than "mayonnaise," there are regulations against soy milk being labeled as "milk." You'll typically see it labeled as "soy beverage."

How Can I Use It?

Soy milk is versatile. You can use it any way that you would ordinarily use cow's milk. It tastes good by itself as a beverage, although some people prefer the flavored varieties. Try them all, then decide which you prefer. You may opt to keep more than one flavor on hand.

In general, it's best to use plain soy milk for baking savory foods such as mashed potatoes. For sweet foods such as cookies, cakes, and pancakes, plain or vanilla soy milk are fine. Carob-flavored soy milk may even work well in some sweet recipes.

• SOY MILK SMOOTHIE •

2 cups fortified vanilla soy milk
1 large, ripe banana
1 cup strawberry halves (fresh or frozen)

Blend all ingredients together in a food processor or blender until smooth.

Yield: Two 12-ounce servings.

Nutritional content per serving: Calories (Kcal): 350, Protein (gm): 7.5, Total Fat (gm): 3.5, Saturated Fat (gm): 0, Cholesterol (mg): 0, Dietary Fiber (gm): 5, Sodium (mg): 95, Calcium (mg): 179, Iron (mg): 2, Zinc (mg): 0

You can also add soy milk to your coffee or tea in place of cream. If you do, pour the soy milk into your cup first, then slowly add the hot beverage, stirring as you go. This will usually prevent the soy milk from curdling, which can sometimes be a problem when it is used in this way.

Here are some other ways to use soy milk. You'll think of many more yourself.

- Pour soy milk over hot cereals such as oatmeal or seven-grain hot cereal with chopped, dried fruit. Use it over cold cereals, too.

- Have a glass of soy milk with your favorite cookies.

- Use soy milk to make custards, puddings, flan, and pie fillings such as pumpkin or cream pie filling.

- Use soy milk to make cream sauces and cream soups.

- Create your own healthy soy-milk shakes and smoothies. Try blending soy milk with any or all of the following: bananas, other fresh fruit, frozen fruit, wheat germ, low-fat frozen yogurt, nondairy-ice cream-substitute, tofu, a few ice cubes, or frozen-fruit-juice cubes.

- Substitute soy milk for cow's milk in recipes for pancakes, waffles, muffins, quick breads, and other baked goods. Soy milk substitutes for cow's milk cup for cup in any recipe that calls for milk.

Nutritional Features
Soy milk is very nutritious. It's a good source of protein, calcium, and iron, and it's rich in phytochemicals—substances that are potentially health supporting and may be important in protecting us against disease. It's also very low in saturated fat and is cholesterol-free.

Nutrients in 8 Ounces of Plain Soy Milk
(Source: 1997 Soyfoods Directory)

	Regular Soy Milk	Lite Soy Milk (reduced fat)
Calories (Kcal):	140	100
Protein (gm):	10	4
Total Fat (gm):	4	2
Carbohydrate (gm):	14	16
Sodium (mg):	120	100
Iron (mg):	1.8	0.6
Riboflavin (mg):	0.1	11
Calcium (mg):	80	80

Which Soy Milk Is Best?

There are many brands of soy milk on the market, and each one tastes a little different than the others. You may need to try several before you hit on the one that you like the best. (My personal favorite is Eden Soy Extra Vanilla.) Not only that, but soy milks vary widely in their nutritional composition, too. Some contain much more fat than others, and even those that are fortified with extra vitamins and minerals vary in the amounts of the nutrients they contain.

The brands of soy milk that are fortified are generally good sources of calcium, vitamin D, riboflavin, and vitamin B_{12}. Examples include Eden Soy Extra and Westbrae Natural West Soy. They provide at least 10 percent of the RDI for those nutrients. Choose a *fortified* soy milk over one that is not fortified, and of those that are fortified, choose a brand that provides at least 25 percent of the RDI for calcium in one cup and at least 10 percent of the RDI for vitamin D, riboflavin, and vitamin B_{12}. Once you've narrowed your choices down to the brands that are the most nutritious, make your final choice based on flavor.

- Soy milk is an excellent alternative to cow's milk for people who are lactose-intolerant, since soy milk contains none of the milk sugar lactose. Soy milk is also a great choice for people who are allergic to the proteins in cow's milk.

- When it comes to feeding infants, don't confuse soy milk with commercial infant formula. Children under the age of one year should be fed breast milk or a commercially prepared infant formula. Commercial infant formulas that are soy-based include Isomil, Prosobee, and Soyalac, to name a few. After the age of one year, regular soy milk is fine, although you should choose a brand that is fortified.

- Some people prefer to use soy milk or another nondairy milk in lieu of milk that comes from the regular supermarket, since milk from standard commercial sources may come from cows that have been treated with the bovine growth hormone BSG (or BST) and been given large amounts of antibiotics. Some brands of cow's milk found in natural foods stores are certified as coming from cows that have not been treated with BSG.

Buying and Storing Soy Milk

You'll find soy milk in natural foods stores and specialty shops, as well as in many supermarkets today. In supermarkets, it's usually found in the Health Foods aisle or in the section with the canned and powdered milks.

If you've never tried soy milk, you may be surprised to learn that it usually *isn't* found in the refrigerated section of the store. Most of the soy milk sold these days is packaged in fluid form in shelf-stable aseptic cartons—either quart or eight-ounce containers. As long as the containers haven't been opened, you can store them in your cupboard for several months before using—check the expiration date on the package. I like to buy soy milk by the case and store it in my cupboard. Not only is it convenient to have a good supply on hand, but the natural foods store where I shop gives me a 10 percent discount on the price when I buy a full case.

At the time of writing, a couple of companies are beginning to sell soy milk or nondairy milk alternatives in the refrigerated case in aseptic containers (which, as I explained before, don't actually need refrigeration) as well as in nonaseptic, one-quart milk cartons. Hopefully, this is a trend that will continue, since many people would logically look in the dairy case for these types of products.

Once opened, soy milk must be refrigerated. Manufacturers say that soy milk will stay fresh in your refrigerator for about five days, although I have kept open containers in my refrigerator for a couple of weeks and not had a problem. When soy milk begins to spoil, it smells sour.

You can buy soy milk in three-packs of eight-ounce aseptic boxes. I find these to be very practical. Not only are they convenient and nutritious for bag lunches or a long day in the car, but they're easy to pack in a bicycle bag or backpack, or in a suitcase for longer trips. When I travel for business, I like to order cereal for breakfast from the room service menu, and I eat it with the soy milk that I've brought from home.

Soy milk can also be purchased as a powder that you mix with water and refrigerate. Most people find it to be less convenient than the kind sold in aseptic packages. If you do buy powdered soy milk, though, store the powder in your refrigerator or freezer to help keep it fresh longer. Some natural foods stores still carry fresh, fluid soy milk as well. It's kept in the refrigerated section of the store (usually near the cow's milk) and sold in quart and half gallon containers.

RICE MILK

What Is It? How Can I Use It?

Rice milk is similar in most ways to soy milk, except that it is made with rice rather than soybeans and is generally not as nutritious. It can be used in all of the same ways as soy milk, and like soy milk, it's usually sold in fluid form in aseptic packages. Like soy milk, it can be found in plain, vanilla, and carob flavors.

Some people like the flavor of rice milk better than soy milk, since it doesn't have the "beanie" aftertaste that some people attribute to the latter. Rice milk also tends to be whiter in color (and looks more like cow's milk) and less viscous; soy milk is tanner in color and a bit creamier in consistency. There is a compromise on the market as well—a soy milk/rice milk blend.

However, in recipes, rice milk and soy milk function virtually identically. Differences in flavors are generally not noticeable when they're used in cooking. You can use whichever you prefer.

Nutritional Features

While some people may like the flavor and color of rice milk better than soy milk, rice milk does not compare favorably to soy milk nutritionally. Take a look at the nutritional composition of one popular brand of rice milk:

Nutrients in 8 Ounces of Rice Milk
(Source: Manufacturer)

	Regular (Plain) Rice Milk	Fortified (Plain) Rice Milk
Calories (Kcal):	120	120
Protein (gm):	1	1
Total Fat (gm):	2	2
Carbohydrate (gm):	25	28
Sodium (mg):	90	90
Iron (mg):	0	0
Riboflavin (mg):	N/A	N/A
Calcium (mg):	16	240

Rice milk is a poor source of protein, calcium, and iron. Fortified rice milk is an excellent source of calcium, but it still lags behind soy milk in other essential nutrients. Rice/soy blends are a good source of protein but are low in calcium, iron, and other vitamins and minerals. At the time of this writing, fortified blends are not available.

In terms of nutrition, it's best to use fortified soy milk most of the time. If you like rice milk or blends, use them occasionally.

• ALMOND APRICOT TAPIOCA PUDDING •

Soaking the tapioca before cooking gives it time to absorb some of the rice milk and helps prevent the tapioca from settling to the bottom of the pan, where it can scorch.

1½ teaspoons EnerG Egg Replacer
2 tablespoons water
¼ cup finely diced dried apricots
½ cup very hot water

¾ cup turbinado sugar
3 tablespoons quick-cooking tapioca
2¾ cup fortified rice milk
1 teaspoon pure almond extract
4 tablespoons toasted, slivered almonds

1. In a small cup, whisk together the egg replacer and water as per package instructions. Set aside.
2. In another small bowl or cup, soak the apricots in hot water.
3. Place sugar, tapioca, rice milk, and egg replacer in a saucepan and stir them together. Let stand 5 minutes.
4. On medium heat, cook the tapioca mixture, stirring constantly, until the mixture comes to a full boil (about 10 minutes). Remove from heat.
5. Stir in the almond extract.
6. Let pudding cool for 20 minutes.
7. Drain apricot pieces and stir them into the pudding.
8. Spoon pudding into 6 serving cups.
9. Sprinkle each cup with 2 teaspoons toasted, slivered almonds.
10. Serve warm or chill in refrigerator before serving.

Makes 6 half-cup servings.

Nutritional content per serving: Calories (Kcal): 79, Protein (gm): 1.5, Total fat (gm): 3.5, Saturated fat (gm): 0, Cholesterol (mg): 0, Dietary fiber (gm): 1, Sodium (mg): 42.5, Calcium (mg): 153, Iron (mg): 0, Zinc (mg): 0

OTHER MILK SUBSTITUTES

Potato, Almond, and Oat Milks

If the idea of replacing cow's milk with milk made from

soybeans or rice seems novel to you, you'll be even more interested to know that milks made from potatoes, almonds, and even oats are also available. All of these have a pleasant, mild flavor and can be used in the same ways as cow's milk. In cooking, all of these are interchangeable, and variations in flavor rarely affect the foods with which they are cooked.

Potato milk (brand name Vegelicious) is packaged in a pouch as a powder—just add water and mix. It's nutritious, but it's not as convenient as the milks available in aseptic packages. One manufacturer is also making oat milk, which is available in aseptic packages but is not as nutrient-dense as soy milk. Almond milk is available in more varieties than either potato or oat milk, but it, too, is not as nutritious as soy milk.

Manufacturers change the formulations of products from time to time. Plus, milk substitutes such as all of those described in this chapter are quickly gaining in popularity, so it's a good bet that there will soon be even more options in stores. For these reasons, you should read and compare the nutrition labels and ingredient listings on products carefully. Products that are not fortified today may be fortified tomorrow.

AISLE 6

COSMETICS   BOOKS

SKIN & HAIR   HERBAL

TOOTHPASTE   HOMEOPATHIC

BATH   VITAMINS

TODAY'S FEATURES: HERBS AND VITAMIN AND MINERAL SUPPLEMENTS

HERBS

What Are They?

According to the Herb Trade Association, an herb is a plant or a component of a plant that is extracted or dried and used for its medicinal or aromatic qualities, or simply because it tastes good. Strictly speaking, though, the botanical term *herb* describes a nonwoody plant that produces seeds and is an annual, which means that at the end of the growing season, it dies.

Herbs are sold in supermarkets and natural foods stores in the form of tea, capsules, extracts, and powders.

How Can I Use Them?

Herbs and preparations made from them have been used widely around the world for centuries, but only recently have mainstream North American health practitioners gotten interested in their therapeutic qualities. Consequently, researchers have only just begun to conduct controlled studies on the use and effectiveness of herbs for a variety of diseases and conditions.

The herb St. John's wort, for instance, is used in Germany for the treatment of depression, anxiety, and insomnia. However, American researchers have only recently initiated controlled studies of its use and effectiveness. We can expect that it will be years before enough data will be available to support recommendations about its use in the U.S.

The same is true for many other popular herbs such as echinacea, evening primrose oil, feverfew, ginkgo biloba, and ginseng, which can be found in several commercial varieties. Since recommendations for the use of herbs are not generally available from mainstream health practitioners, you'll have to look to reliable alternative practitioners for information about which herbs are safe to use and in what doses. Some references are listed in the next section of this chapter.

Many herbs have therapeutic effects and appear to be useful in treating high blood lipid levels, gastrointestinal disorders, respiratory and urinary tract problems, sleep disorders, anxiety, depression, cold sores, and cold and flu symptoms. Some herbs may also boost the efficiency of your immune system and help to protect against cancer. However, others can be toxic, and many herbs that are safe in small quantities can be unsafe in larger amounts. For this reason, it's vital that you have reliable information about the safety of herbs that you might be considering using.

Buying and Storing Herbs

Store herbs and herbal preparations in a cool, dry place out of direct sunlight.

Recommended Resources About Herbs

The American Botanical Council and *HerbalGram* magazine
P.O. Box 201660
Austin, TX 78720
Phone 512-331-8868; fax 512-331-1924.
Available at natural foods stores and by subscription; $25 for four issues, $45 for eight issues, $60 for twelve issues.
E-mail: custserv@herbalgram.org
Internet address: http://www.herbalgram.org

The Use and Safety of Common Herbs and Herbal Teas, 2nd Edition (1996). By Winston J. Craig, Ph.D., R.D., Professor of Nutrition, Andrews University, Michigan, 49104. Paperback, 75 pages. This book is available from Golden Harvest Books, 4610 Lisa Lane, Berrien Springs, Michigan 49103. Phone 616-471-3351, fax 616-471-3485, or e-mail wcraig@andrews.edu. Send a check or money order in the amount of $11.45, which includes shipping within the U.S. and Canada.

The Honest Herbal: A Sensible Guide to the Use of Herbs and Related Remedies, 3rd Edition. By Tyler E. Varro, Ph.D. Paperback, 375 pages. Published by Lubrecht & Cramer Ltd.; ISBN: 1560242876. List price $18.95 at bookstores.

VITAMIN AND MINERAL SUPPLEMENTS

What Are They?

A full-scale discussion of supplements would merit a volume of its own and is beyond the scope of this book. Suffice to say that natural foods stores carry supplements of individual vitamins and minerals as well as multivitamin and mineral combinations. Gelatin capsules are common in natural brands, but more manufacturers are using vegicaps now, since most vegetarians won't use capsules made with animal-derived gelatin.

The vitamins and minerals that you'll find in any store are actually only a sampling of the hundreds and thousands of substances naturally present in whole foods and necessary for optimal health. Those that you'll find on store shelves are the ones that have been identified. We now know that there are probably many, many more that have not yet been discovered.

Beyond the vitamins and minerals that have long been known to exist in foods of both plant and animal origin, there is a wide array of other beneficial substances that exist in plants. As a group, these are called *phytochemicals*—plant constituents that have biological activity in humans and protect our health. Carotenoids such as beta-carotene and lycopene, isoflavones such as genistein (a form of plant estrogen), and many others are becoming more familiar to scientists, nutritionists, and consumers alike. It's humbling for a nutritionist to recognize that the science of nutrition is in its infancy. There is a still a great deal that we don't know about how nutrients work in our bodies and how individual nutrients interact with each other. For that reason, it's difficult to advise people about the proper use of supplements.

How Can I Use Them?

Should I take a supplement? What should I take, and how much? I hear these questions all the time, and I still have difficulty giving an answer.

The experts are split on the issue of supplements—which ones, how much, for whom? There are valid differences of opinion, since the science is still so new. Some nutrition scientists recommend a multivitamin mineral supplement as "insurance" for the cola-and-french-fries crowd, while others say it's better to push the idea of getting what you need from whole foods. Under certain conditions, the experts do agree, however. For instance, the idea that women who are considering pregnancy take a folic acid supplement—which has been shown to reduce the incidence of neural tube defects in newborns—has been widely accepted.

In my opinion (one shared by many, but not all), the argument for taking supplements for the general, healthy public is best supported for the antioxidant nutrients—vitamins A, C, and E, selenium, and mixed carotenes (as opposed to beta-carotene alone). We are exposed to more environmental contaminants that ever today, and it's possible that antioxidants in amounts we couldn't get from an ordinary, healthful diet, may help reduce the production of harmful free radicals.

Do I take supplements myself? At this time I do not. I'm one of the die-hard "get it from whole foods" advocates. This is my personal choice, and yours may be different. At this time there's really no right or wrong approach.

My goal has always been to eat the healthiest diet as consistently as I can. I put my efforts into eating well, getting plenty of sleep and fluids, and exercising regularly. For people who know they don't eat well, though, and don't think they'll change, it may be wise to take a regular multivitamin mineral supplement (as opposed to high-potency formulas) and additional antioxidants. But while you're at it, why not aim for several big servings of fruits and/or vegetables every day? Just in case.

Supplements: Which Ones and How Much?

I generally like Dr. Andrew Weil's approach to the issue of dietary supplementation. For more assistance with the questions of "which ones" and "how much," I suggest reading two of his books: *Spontaneous Healing,* New York: Ballantine Books, 1996; and *Eight Weeks to Optimum Health,* New York: Knopf, 1997. You can pick these books up in any library or bookstore. You can also go to Dr. Weil's Web site, drweil.com

AISLE 7

DAIRY AND REFRIGERATED

TODAY'S FEATURES:
SOY CHEESE, TOFU, TEMPEH, AND MISO

The soybean. That amazing little bean can be used to make so many foods. What used to be the butt of jokes is now the darling of the food industry since its many nutritional and health-promoting qualities are being recognized worldwide. Among the many foods that are made from soybeans:

Soy nuts
Soy sauce
Soynut butter
Soy-based infant formulas
Soybean oil
Meat analogs (substitutes for sausage, cold cuts, hot dogs, and hamburgers)
Soy grits
Miso
Soy flour

Nondairy frozen novelties and ice cream substitutes
Soy milk
Canned soybeans

The lists goes on. The soy foods featured in this aisle—soy cheese, tofu, tempeh, and miso (along with the soy milk described in Aisle 5)—are the foods that newcomers to natural foods ask me about most often.

SOY CHEESE

What Is It?
It's similar to regular cheese, but it's made with soy milk instead of cow's milk. The label will call it "cheese alternative." (One brand, Almond Rella, is made with almond milk instead of cow's milk.) Cheese alternatives come in different varieties and flavors, including mozzarella-style, Cheddar-style, cream cheese, sour cream, Parmesan cheese, and others. Brands I've used and liked include Soya Kaas, Soyco Foods, Soymage, Tofu Rella, and Tofutti.

How Can I Use It?
Use it in all the same ways that you would use cheese made from cow's milk. Mozzarella-style soy cheese works well on pizzas. Use soy cream cheese on bagels and in recipes, use soy sour cream to make dips and salad dressings, and sprinkle soy Parmesan cheese onto baked potatoes, pasta, and salads.

• SPINACH AND MUSHROOM PIZZA •

A couple slices of this pizza with a mixed green salad or a bowl of fresh fruit salad makes a filling meal. This recipe makes enough dough for two pizza crusts. You can double the topping to make two large pizzas, or you can save half of the dough for another time. Pizza dough will keep in the refrigerator, wrapped tightly, for a few days, or frozen for several weeks.

WHOLE WHEAT PIZZA DOUGH

1½ teaspoons yeast
1 tablespoon honey or sugar
1¾ cup warm water
1 teaspoon olive oil
1 teaspoon salt or less
2 cups whole wheat flour
2 cups unbleached white flour

PIZZA TOPPING

¾ cup bottled, seasoned organic pasta sauce (more or less to suit your taste)
1 cup shredded, mozzarella-style nondairy cheese
½ cup frozen, chopped spinach (thawed and drained well)
½ cup fresh or canned mushroom slices
Soy parmesan cheese, if desired

1. Preheat oven to 375 degrees F.
2. In a large mixing bowl, dissolve the yeast in warm water (about 110 degrees F) and add honey or sugar. Add oil and salt and stir.
3. Gradually add flour, alternating between whole wheat and white. Mix well after each addition using a wooden spoon or your hands to make a soft dough.
4. Turn out dough onto a floured board and knead for 5 minutes, adding more flour if needed.
5. Oil the sides of the mixing bowl lightly. Put the dough into the bowl, turn the dough over once, cover with a towel or waxed paper, and let set in a warm place for about 30 minutes.

6. Divide the dough in half. Reserve one half for later if desired (store in refrigerator or freezer).

7. Spread dough on a 14-inch pizza pan. You can roll the dough out first on a floured surface or simply press the ball of dough onto the pizza pan and distribute evenly using your hands.

8. Spoon on pizza sauce and spread to within a half inch of edges of dough.

9. Sprinkle shredded cheese evenly across the pizza.

10. Add spinach and mushroom toppings, distributing vegetables evenly over the pizza.

11. Place pizza in the oven and bake for 30–40 minutes, until crust and/or cheese begins to brown lightly. Do not overcook.

12. Remove from oven and let set for 2–3 minutes before serving.

Cut into slices and serve. Sprinkle soy Parmesan-style cheese on top of pizza slices as desired.

Makes 2 large pizzas (about 8 slices per pizza).

Nutrient content per slice: Calories (Kcal): 293, Protein (gm): 15.5, Total fat (gm): 2.5, Saturated fat (gm): 0, Cholesterol (mg): 0, Dietary fiber (gm): 5, Sodium (mg): 635 (less if less table salt is added), Calcium (mg): 44, Iron (mg): 2, Zinc (mg): 1

Soy cheese is a useful product for people who typically eat lots of cheese but want to lower their saturated-fat-and-cholesterol intakes. You might think that soy cheese would appeal to vegans, or strict vegetarians who eat no animal products (including animal by-products) but many brands actually contain animal ingredients such as casein, a cow's milk protein. The casein is added to give the soy cheese the characteristic "stretchiness" of dairy cheese when it's melted. People want alternatives to dairy cheese, but most still want the cheese to taste and function like regular cheese.

....

The 1998 U.S. Soyfoods Directory is a wealth of information about all aspects of soy foods. It gives descriptions of soy foods, including their nutritional composition, recipes, and the companies that produce and distribute the products. For a copy of the Directory, call 1-800-TALK-SOY. A searchable version of the Directory is available on the Internet at: http://www.soyfoods.com/

....

Nutritional Features

Soy cheeses have pros and cons nutritionally. They are not necessarily lower in total fat than dairy cheeses, and some are actually higher. Some are higher in sodium than dairy cheeses, and others are approximately the same. Soy cheeses are usually, but not always, similar in protein content to dairy cheeses, and they are similar to or even higher in calcium.

Soy cheeses contain no cholesterol, and they are free of or much lower in saturated fat. That's important, since about two thirds of the fat in dairy cheese is saturated fat. For anyone who is trying to reduce their intake of animal fats and cholesterol and become less dependent on using cheese in recipes, soy cheeses can be a helpful transition food.

The nutritional comparisons between soy and dairy cheeses vary, depending upon the variety of cheese. Here are a few examples, for comparison:

Nutritional Comparison of
One Ounce Dairy and Soy Cheddar-Style Cheeses
(Source: Manufacturer)

	Organic Valley Sharp Cheddar	Soymage Cheddar Alternative
Calories (Kcal):	110	60
Protein (gm):	7	2
Total fat (gm):	9	3
Saturated fat (gm):	6	0
Cholesterol (mg):	25	0
Sodium (mg):	190	340
Calcium (mg):	200	250

Nutritional Comparison of 2 Tablespoons of Dairy
and Soy Cream Cheeses
(Source: Manufacturer)

	Organic Valley Organic Cream Cheese	Soya Kaas Plain Cream Cheese Style
Calories (Kcal):	100	100
Protein (gm):	2	3
Total fat (gm):	9	9
Saturated fat (gm):	6	1.5
Cholesterol (mg):	30	0
Sodium (mg):	100	110
Calcium (mg):	20	N/A

Nutritional Comparison of One Ounce
Dairy and Soy Mozzarella-Style Cheeses
(Source: Manufacturer)

	Organic Valley Part-Skim Mozzarella	Soymage Mozzarella Style
Calories (Kcal):	80	60
Protein (gm):	8	2
Total fat (gm):	5	3
Saturated fat (gm):	3	0
Cholesterol (mg):	16	0
Sodium (mg):	170	340
Calcium (mg):	200	250

Soy cheeses might also be appealing for people who want to boost their intake of the protective phytochemicals found in soy foods *(see the discussion of supplements in Aisle 6 for more information about phytochemicals)*. For people who are lactose-intolerant, soy cheeses may be helpful. Most people who are lactose-intolerant can tolerate small amounts of hard cheeses such as Cheddar, Swiss, and Parmesan, but for those who can't, soy cheeses are a great find.

Some people go to natural foods stores for *rennetless* cheese. Rennet is an enzyme that comes from the stomach lining of calves, pigs, lambs, or baby goats and is used to coagulate ripened dairy cheeses. Vegetarians avoid cheese made with rennet. Natural foods stores typically carry a good selection of rennetless cheeses, which aren't easy to find at regular supermarkets.

To be sure that a cheese has not been coagulated with rennet, the product label should say that a vegetable enzyme was used. Soft cheeses such as cottage cheese, ricotta cheese, and cream cheese are not ripened but may have been made with rennet to produce a firmer product.

Buying and Storing Soy Cheese

Soy cheese, like dairy cheese, should be stored in the refrigerator. It keeps for about the same length of time as dairy cheese—a couple of weeks to several months, depending upon the type of cheese.

TOFU

What Is It?

Tofu is soybean curd. It's made much the same way that cheese is made by using a coagulant to curdle soy milk (rennet isn't used to make tofu), separating the liquid from the solids, then pressing the solids into a block. A slightly different process is used to make silken tofu (see Buying and Storing Tofu, page 121).

Tofu looks like a white block of spongy cheese. It has little odor or flavor but picks up the flavor of whatever it's cooked with.

How Can I Use It?

Tofu is almost infinitely versatile. Most people think of it as the rubbery little stir-fried cubes in Buddha's Delight (mixed Chinese vegetables) at Chinese restaurants, but I use tofu even more often for making puddings and pie fillings, sandwich fillings, and baked goods.

• SUNDAY MORNING BLUEBERRY MUFFINS •

Did you know that you can use ¼ cup of tofu to replace one egg in recipes? Blend the tofu with the liquid ingredients in the recipe. This substitution works especially well in baked goods.

¼ cup tofu (to replace 1 egg in original recipe)
½ cup soy milk
¼ cup vegetable oil
1½ cups unbleached, all-purpose flour
½ cup turbinado sugar
2 teaspoons baking powder
½ teaspoon salt
1 cup fresh blueberries or ¾ cup thawed, frozen blueberries

Preheat oven to 400 degrees F. Line 12 muffin cups with paper liners or grease well. In a mixing bowl, combine tofu, soy milk, and oil; blend well. Mix in remaining ingredients just until moistened. Gently fold in blueberries.

Fill muffin cups ⅔ full. Bake 20 to 25 minutes or until lightly browned. Remove immediately from muffin tin.

Makes 12 muffins.

Nutrient content per muffin: Calories (Kcal): 149, Protein (gm): 3, Total fat (gm): 5, Saturated fat (gm): 1, Cholesterol (mg): 0, Dietary fiber (gm): 1, Sodium (mg): 151, Calcium (mg): 31, Iron (mg): 1, Zinc (mg): 0

The best way to see for yourself how versatile tofu can be is to try your hand at fixing a few recipes. There are some excellent soy cookbooks available at the library or bookstore. A few of my favorites are:

- *Tofu Cookery*, revised edition, by Louise Hagler, Summertown, TN: The Book Publishing Company, 1991. This oversized, softcover book is a classic. The photos alone are worth the cost of the book.

- *Soy of Cooking*; by Marie Oser, Minneapolis: Chronimed Publishing, 1996.

- *The Complete Soy Cookbook*, by Paulette Mitchell, New York: Macmillan, 1998.

To inspire you about ways in which you might use tofu, here is a sampling of some of my favorites:

Quiche
Cheesecake
Tofu "scrambled eggs"
Baked, marinated tofu
Mock egg salad *(see Aisle 4)*
Maple walnut bagel spread (for my bagels! *Recipe on page 122*)
Whipped topping for pies and berries *(see page 125)*
Pumpkin pie filling *(see page 125)*
Vegetable dips
Vegetable lasagna filling
Chocolate- or banana-cream-pie filling
Manicotti or stuffed shells filling

Nutritional Features

Tofu is rich in protein. Regular tofu is moderately high in fat, although "lite" versions are now available. Tofu is cholesterol-free and low in sodium, and even regular tofu is very low in saturated fat. Like other soy foods, tofu is packed with beneficial phytochemicals. Some forms are high in calcium, depending upon the coagulant used in processing. Tofu coagulated with calcium phosphate, for instance, is higher in calcium than tofu processed with nigari (a type of sea vegetable).

Tofu is nutritious, so it's a great addition to your diet. But the other advantage to using tofu is that it can *displace* dairy products, eggs, and meat, and in doing so, it reduces your total intake of cholesterol and saturated fat.

Nutrient Composition of Tofu
(Source: 1998 U.S. Soyfoods Directory)

	Tofu, raw, firm ($^1/_2$ cup = 126 grams)	Tofu, raw, regular ($^1/_2$ cup = 124 grams)
Serving size:	69.8 gm	84.6 gm
Calories (Kcal):	145	76
Protein (gm):	15.8	8.1
Total fat (gm):	8.7	4.8
Saturated fat (gm):	N/A	N/A
Cholesterol (mg):	0	0
Sodium (mg):	14	7
Calcium (mg):	205	105

Buying and Storing Tofu

Tofu Comes in Different Forms

If you've shopped for tofu, you've probably noticed that there are different types—soft, firm, extra firm, silken. You may have also noticed that tofu is sometimes packed in water-filled plastic containers, in aseptic cartons, or even vacuum-packed in plastic.

The different forms of tofu result from the degree to which water has been removed. Soft tofu, for instance, contains the most water. It's the easiest to blend into drinks, dips, or spreads. Firm tofu is, well, a little firmer or more dense. It has more water pressed out of it than does soft tofu. Extra-firm tofu is the densest. It holds up well when it's jostled around in a stir-fry. Serious cooks who are particular about the texture of their finished products may differentiate between the various types of tofu, but many of us regular folks just keep firm tofu on hand for everyday use, since it works well in just about any recipe.

• MAPLE WALNUT BAGEL SPREAD •

1/3 cup raisins
1/2 cup very hot water
1/2 pound (225 grams) firm tofu
1/4 cup plain soy yogurt
1/2 cup pure maple syrup
1/2 teaspoon ground cinnamon
1 tablespoon tahini
2 teaspoons vanilla
2 teaspoons whole wheat flour
1/3 cup chopped walnuts

Preheat oven to 350 degrees F. Oil a 1-quart baking dish or casserole. Place raisins into a small dish or cup and pour hot water over them. Set aside to soak.

Place tofu, yogurt, maple syrup, cinnamon, tahini, vanilla, and whole wheat flour into a blender or food processor. Blend well, stopping frequently to scrape sides of blender. Turn the ingredients over with a spatula if necessary for thorough blending.

Drain raisins, then chop them into small pieces. Add raisins and walnuts to the tofu mixture and mix. Pour mixture into baking dish and bake, uncovered, for 40 minutes or until set.

Makes 2 cups of spread.

Nutrient content per ¼ cup serving: Calories (Kcal): 172, Protein (gm): 7, Total fat (gm): 6, Saturated fat (gm): 0.5, Cholesterol (mg): 0, Dietary fiber (gm): 1, Sodium (mg): 42, Calcium (mg): 78, Iron (mg): 4, Zinc (mg): 1

Years ago, tofu was sold two ways in natural foods stores: already packed in water-filled plastic containers, or in bulk barrels from which you fished out your own block. It is still commonly sold in water-filled containers, but now it's also found in aseptic packages that look like little bricks or blocks. The tofu sold in aseptic packages is made from a slightly different process than that used to make water-packed tofu. Tofu sold in aseptic containers is actually coagulated right inside the container itself. It has a smoother, more custardy texture and is labeled "silken" tofu. It, too, comes in soft, firm, and extra-firm densities. The choice of which type to use is a matter of personal preference.

You'll also find ready-made tofu dishes for sale in the refrigerator case, such as baked tofu and tofu that has been marinated in sauces or spices. You can just heat and serve these products, which can be a good way to try tofu if you've never before tasted it.

Storing Tofu

Personally, my favorite type of tofu is Mori-Nu brand in the aseptic packages. That's because I never know when I'm going to feel like using it, and tofu packaged this way will keep for several months without refrigeration. After the container is opened, any leftover tofu has to be refrigerated.

If you buy tofu packed in water, it will keep in your refrigerator for about two weeks. (Nasoya and White Wave are two national brands carried by most natural foods stores.) After you open the package, you'll need to rinse any tofu that you don't use and store it in a bowl or container of water. It will keep for about a week in your refrigerator. You are supposed to rinse it daily with clean water to keep the tofu fresh. I have to admit that when I did buy tofu in this form, I rarely rinsed it daily, and it kept fresh nevertheless for about one week. You'll know when tofu is spoiling, because it gradually turns yellowish in color and begins to smell sour.

You can also freeze tofu for several months. Many people freeze tofu for the effect that freezing has on its texture. Thawed, the tofu has a chewier, more rubbery texture that some people feel resembles the texture of meat. It can then be used in recipes, such as chili, stews, and casseroles, as a meat substitute.

Tofu that is vacuum-packed is usually the prepared style, such as barbecued tofu or other marinated varieties. Once the vacuum pack is opened, leftovers should be kept in the refrigerator for not more than about one week.

• PUMPKIN PUDDING WITH TOFU WHIPPED TOPPING •

This is really two separate recipes. The first, pumpkin pudding, can be used as a pie filling as well as a pudding. I like to bake it in a casserole dish, because it's quicker than preparing a piecrust to go with it, and forgoing the crust saves calories—not an insignificant factor, considering the amount of this dish that you may eat. Be forewarned: this pudding is good, and you won't be able to stop at one dish!

The Tofu Whipped Topping is a nice accompaniment to the pudding; it's versatile and can be used with other desserts as well. I like to spoon it onto cups of fresh berries.

PUMPKIN PUDDING

8 ounces of firm tofu
One 15-ounce can of pumpkin pie filling
5 tablespoons of honey or maple syrup
3 tablespoons of molasses
½ teaspoon powdered ginger
1 teaspoon cinnamon
¼ teaspoon nutmeg
1 tablespoon whole wheat or soy flour

Preheat the oven to 350 degrees F. Combine all of the ingredients in a blender or mixing bowl and blend until smooth. Stop occasionally to scrape down the sides of the blender or bowl. Pour into a lightly oiled 8-inch-by-8-inch baking pan or a 1½ quart casserole and bake for about 40 minutes. Let cool completely before serving (best if chilled before serving).

Yield: About 6 servings.

Nutrient content per serving: Calories (Kcal): 228, Protein (gm): 7, Total fat (gm): 3.5, Saturated fat (gm): 1, Cholesterol (mg): 0, Dietary fiber (gm): 1, Sodium (mg): 231, Calcium (mg): 192

TOFU WHIPPED TOPPING

4 tablespoons of cashews (salted)
½ cup water
16 ounces of firm tofu
6 tablespoons of maple syrup
2 teaspoons vanilla
¼ teaspoon cinnamon

Grind the nuts in a spice mill, blender, or food processor until very fine. Combine the pulverized nuts and water in a small dish or cup and whisk them together to make cashew milk.

In a blender, process the tofu, maple syrup, vanilla, cinnamon, and about half of the cashew milk. Blend until smooth. Use additional cashew milk if necessary for blending; the amount you'll need may depend upon the type of tofu you use and how smooth or dry it is. Chill thoroughly.

Yield: About 2½ cups.

Nutrients per ¼ cup: Calories (Kcal): 125, Protein (gm): 13, Total fat (gm): 9, Saturated fat (gm): 1, Cholesterol (mg): 0, Dietary fiber (gm): 1, Sodium (mg): 58, Calcium (mg): 168

TEMPEH

What Is It?

I meet plenty of people who are afraid to try tofu. Why, I can never understand. Tofu is so bland, so benign. But tempeh? I admit I was intimidated by tempeh myself, primarily because of its unsightly appearance.

Tempeh is a traditional Indonesian soy food made from whole soybeans. Sometimes it's mixed with a grain, such as rice. It's a fermented product that is usually pressed into the shape of a flat, rectangular block—a cultured bean cake. In the natural foods store, you'll usually find it vacuum-packed in plastic. Tempeh looks like a lumpy, bumpy, brownish, flat slab. It's not a pretty sight, but its versatility and nutritional profile turned me into a convert.

How Can I Use It?

Like tofu, tempeh is relatively bland and picks up the flavor of foods that it's cooked with. You can use tempeh as a substitute for meat in soups, stews, casseroles, and chili—just crumble it in. You can marinate it. You can grill it. You can use it in many of the same ways that people use meat.

Nutritional Features

Tempeh is rich in protein, just like tofu. It's also a good source of riboflavin, thiamin, niacin, calcium, iron, and zinc.

Nutrient Composition of 55 Grams of Tempeh (½ cup = 83 grams)

(Source: 1998 U.S. Soyfoods Directory)

Calories (Kcal):	199
Protein (gm):	19
Total fat (gm):	7.7
Saturated fat (gm):	N/A
Cholesterol (mg):	0
Sodium (mg):	6
Riboflavin (mg):	0.11
Thiamin (mg):	0.13
Niacin (mg):	4.63
Calcium (mg):	93
Iron (mg):	2.26
Zinc (mg):	1.81

Buying and Storing Tempeh

You'll find tempeh in both the frozen foods section and the refrigerator section of the natural foods store. Lightlife and White Wave are two national brands that you'll commonly see.

Tempeh comes in several varieties, depending upon the grains and/or other ingredients with which it was mixed. It keeps for about a week or two in the refrigerator or for several months in the freezer. You can also find ready-made tempeh products such as tempeh sloppy-joe filling or barbecued tempeh. These products can be a good way to try tempeh for the first time if you've never tasted it before. Like plain tempeh, these products keep for a week or two in the refrigerator or they can be frozen.

• BASIC TEMPEH SALAD •

This recipe is versatile. You can use Basic Tempeh Salad as a sandwich filling (similar to chicken salad or tuna salad) on bread or in a pita pocket, or you can use it to stuff tomatoes for cold tomato salad.

8 ounces tempeh, any variety
1/2 cup celery, chopped finely (leaves and stem)
1/4 cup green onion, chopped
1/4 cup soy mayonnaise (more or less to suit your taste)
2 teaspoons yellow mustard
1 teaspoon soy sauce
1/2 teaspoon garlic powder
1/4 teaspoon turmeric

Steam the tempeh over a pot of boiling water (or in a vegetable steamer) for 20 minutes. This will make the tempeh soft enough to work with. Cool completely, then cut or break into small pieces in a medium-sized bowl.

While the tempeh is cooling, chop the celery and onions and set aside. Whisk together the mayonnaise, mustard, soy sauce, garlic powder, and turmeric in a small dish.

Once the tempeh has cooled, add the chopped vegetables and mayonnaise mixture and toss everything together well. Cover and chill before serving.

Yield: About 2 cups.

Nutrient content per ½ cup serving: Calories (Kcal): 122, Protein (gm): 3, Total fat (gm): 8, Saturated fat (gm): 1.5, Cholesterol (mg): 0, Dietary fiber (gm): 1, Sodium (mg): 185, Calcium (mg): 34

You'll also find free-range eggs in the refrigerator section of the store. Free-range eggs are eggs from chickens that have been allowed to move freely rather than being confined. These eggs have been produced more humanely than those from chickens raised in factory farms. All eggs are superconcentrated in cholesterol, though, regardless of how the chickens were treated.

MISO

What Is It?
Miso is a traditional, fermented Japanese condiment made from soybeans, salt, a mold culture, and possibly a grain such as rice. These ingredients are aged for a period of one to three years. Miso is made in a variety of flavors and colors, depending upon the ingredients used and the amount of time that the miso is aged.

How Can I Use It?
In Japan, miso is mixed with hot water to make miso soup, where it is commonly served for breakfast. It can be also be used to flavor or season many other foods, including soups

and sauces. In some recipes, miso can be substituted for salt or soy sauce.

• MISO SOUP •

(Reprinted with permission from the 1997 U.S. Soyfoods Directory)

Miso soup is a traditional morning food in Japan. Try it and you'll see why. You can sip miso soup anytime as a plain broth or you can add small bits of chopped sea vegetables and/or tofu, depending upon your mood and what you have on hand.

1 teaspoon soybean oil
2 cloves garlic, mashed
½ cup onions, sliced lengthwise
1 teaspoon fresh ginger root, grated
½ cup carrots, thinly sliced
1 cup mushrooms, thinly sliced
2 tablespoons miso
1 tablespoon dry sherry, to taste
¼ cup plus 3¾ cups water

Heat oil in medium saucepan over medium heat. Add garlic and onions; sauté until soft. Add fresh ginger root, carrots and mushrooms. Cook an additional 5–10 minutes, or until vegetables are crisp tender.

Dissolve miso in ¼ cup of the water and add it to the vegetables in the saucepan along with the remaining water and dry sherry. Reheat and serve.

Serves 6.

Nutrient content per serving (1 cup): Calories (Kcal): 32, Protein
(gm): 1, Total fat (gm): 1, Dietary fiber (gm): 1, Sodium (mg): 236

Nutritional Features
Miso is very high in sodium, so use it sparingly. It's high in
flavor, though, so you won't have to use much.

Nutrient Content of 1 Tablespoon of Miso
(Source: Pennington. *Food Values of Portions Commonly
Used*, 15th Edition)

Calories (Kcal):	35.5
Protein (gm):	2
Total fat (gm):	1
Saturated fat (gm):	0
Cholesterol (mg):	0
Dietary fiber (gm):	0
Sodium (mg):	629
Calcium (mg):	11.5
Iron (mg):	0.5
Zinc (mg):	0.6

AISLE 8

FROZEN FOODS

TODAY'S FEATURES: NONDAIRY FROZEN NOVELTIES AND ICE CREAM SUBSTITUTES, FROZEN ENTRÉES

NONDAIRY FROZEN NOVELTIES AND ICE CREAM SUBSTITUTES

What Are They?

If you want a sweet, frozen, ice cream–like dessert, but you want to avoid the saturated fat and cholesterol found in regular ice cream, you'll find lots of choices in natural foods stores. These products are also great for people who are lactose-intolerant, and most are appropriate for vegans, who eat no animal products at all.

Sorbet-style nondairy frozen desserts are made primarily from fruit juice or frozen fruit. They contain no refined sugars. Examples include Cascadian Farms Blackberry Sorbet and Tofutti Orange Peach Mango Sorbet. Others are creamy, like ice cream. They're usually made with a soybean or tofu base, such as Tofutti Better Pecan, or there's Imagine's brown rice–based Rice Dream, with flavors like Cookies 'n

Dream and Cappuccino Rice Dream. Sweet Nothings is a brand based on brown rice syrup and fruit juice concentrate. Flavors include Espresso Fudge and Very Berry Blueberry. All of these nondairy frozen desserts come in novelty styles, too, such as pops, bars, pies, and cones.

How Can I Use Them?
Enjoy them in all the usual ways. Serve a scoop with a bowl of berries or fresh fruit salad. Use nondairy frozen desserts to make fresh fruit smoothies and shakes. Press a scoop between two oatmeal cookies to make an ice cream sandwich.

• OLD-FASHIONED CHOCOLATE MALT •

¾ cup fortified soy milk (plain, vanilla, or carob)
½ cup chocolate nondairy frozen dessert (such as Rice Dream or Tofutti)
1 tablespoon malt powder

Place all ingredients into a blender and mix on high speed until smooth. Pour into a tall glass and serve immediately.

Makes 1 serving.

Nutritional content per serving: Calories (Kcal): 243, Protein (gm): 5.5, Total fat (gm): 7, Saturated fat (gm): 0, Cholesterol (mg): 0, Dietary fiber (gm): 0, Sodium (mg): 148, Calcium (mg): 150, Iron (mg): 1, Zinc (mg): 0.3

Make your own nondairy frozen dessert using nothing but bananas. Just take ripe bananas, peel them, and place them in airtight plastic bags in the freezer. Once they're frozen, you can run them through your juicer (the heavy-

duty kind, like Champion brand) or process them in a
heavy-duty blender. This makes a creamy banana soft-
serve style "ice cream" that you'll swear is made with real
dairy cream. You can toss in a few strawberries or blueberries for some variation in flavor. This stuff is so good, it's
the sole reason I bought my Vita Mixer (a heavy-duty
blender). If you don't want to invest in a juicer or heavy-
duty blender, just eat the frozen bananas "as is." They're
great!

Nutritional Features
Nondairy frozen desserts compare favorably with ice cream
in that they are much lower in saturated fat and contain no
cholesterol. Some are fat-free, some are not. Take a look at
how some nondairy frozen desserts compare in nutritional
composition with premium ice cream:

Nutritional Comparisons of a Half Cup of Ice Cream with Half Cup Portions of Nondairy Frozen Desserts
(Source: Manufacturer)

	Ben and Jerry's Butter Pecan	Imagine Foods Cappuccino Rice Dream
Calories (Kcal):	310	130
Protein (gm):	5	1
Total fat (gm):	25	5
Saturated fat (gm):	11	N/A
Cholesterol (mg):	85	0
Sodium (mg):	125	80
Calcium (mg):	100	N/A

	Sweet Nothings Espresso Fudge	Tofutti Better Pecan
Calories (Kcal):	130	220
Protein (gm):	0	1
Total fat (gm):	0	13
Saturated fat (gm):	0	0
Cholesterol (mg):	0	0
Sodium (mg):	10	200
Calcium (mg):	0	N/A

	Cascadian Farms Blackberry Sorbet	Tofutti Raspberry Tea Sorbet
Calories (Kcal):	90	80
Protein (gm):	0	0
Total fat (gm):	0	0
Saturated fat (gm):	0	0
Cholesterol (mg):	0	0
Sodium (mg):	76	2
Calcium (mg):	N/A	N/A

Buying and Storing Nondairy Frozen Novelties and Ice Cream Substitutes

Nondairy ice creams should be used within one to two weeks if they have been thawed and refrozen.

FROZEN ENTRÉES

What Are They?

Well, they run the gamut from adzuki beans and rice to Yucatán-style burritos. They include all-American pot pies, pizza, and vegetarian-style meat-loaf-and-mashed-potato dinners as well as a long line of ethnic meals. Some popular brands that I like include Amy's, Cascadian Farm, Hain, Jaclyn's, Natural Touch, Ruthie's Foods, and many others.

How Can I Use Them? (Why Are They Special?)

I'm including a discussion of frozen entrées in this beginner's guide to natural foods for two reasons:

The Familiarity Factor

Trying ready-made foods that incorporate unfamiliar ingredients is a good way for people who are new to natural foods to sample foods that they've never before tasted. The added advantage here is that the ready-made foods are likely to be good examples of how an unfamiliar dish *should* taste. That way, if you later decide to make the dish at home from scratch yourself, you'll have a standard with which to compare it. If you've never tasted adzuki beans or couscous or tofu or soy cheese, here's your chance.

I also like to encourage people to try healthy foods from other cultures. Buying frozen ethnic-style entrées is, once again, a good way to experiment with unfamiliar foods and, ultimately, to add variety to your diet. I found it much easier myself to eat more whole grains and vegetables when I expanded my range of choices to plant-based ethnic entrées. So, if you've never eaten a tamale or empanada or tasted Indian curried vegetables, head to a natural foods store and try an ethnic-style frozen meal.

They're Better for You

Maybe you've noticed how much aisle space is devoted to frozen entrées at the regular supermarket. That's because many people depend on ready-made products for their weekday meals. Maybe they cook on weekends, and maybe not, but during the week many people are simply too busy to fix a meal from scratch. So they pop a frozen dinner into the oven or microwave, or they go out to eat.

If you depend heavily on frozen entrées, then you will

find a greater number of healthful choices at the natural foods store. Regular supermarkets are carrying more natural-foods-brand frozen entrées as well, but the selection is still dwarfed by the mainstream brands. Frozen entrées made by natural foods companies more consistently contain more dietary fiber, less sodium, less saturated fat, and less cholesterol. They don't contain artificial flavorings and colorings, and they don't contain such ingredients as monosodium glutamate, hydrogenated oils, and other additives that are so often seen in commercial brands.

When you buy a frozen entrée or dinner, does the amount of food inside the box seem like a child's portion? If so, round out the meal with a mixed green salad, a baked potato, a slice of whole-grain bread or a whole-grain roll, and/or some fresh fruit.

Nutritional Features
The nutritional composition of natural food frozen entrées varies widely from product to product. To quickly scan and compare the nutritional compositions of several dozen products, refer to my book *The Vegetarian Food Guide and Nutrition Counter* (Berkley Books, 1997).

Generally, when you choose frozen entrées, read the nutrition labels and choose those that are lowest in saturated fat, cholesterol, and sodium, and highest in dietary fiber. (The table on page 139 shows how several products compare nutritionally.)

Nutrient Composition of Selected Frozen Entrées
(Source: Manufacturer)

	Amy's Black Bean and Vegetable Enchilada	Amy's Macaroni and Soy Cheese
Serving size:	9.5 oz.	9 oz.
Calories (Kcal):	130	360
Protein (gm):	4	14
Total fat (gm):	4	14
Saturated fat (gm):	0	1
Cholesterol (mg):	0	0
Dietary fiber (gm):	2	4
Sodium (mg):	390	500
Calcium (mg):	N/A	N/A
Iron (mg):	N/A	N/A

	Amy's Tofu Vegetable Lasagna	Cascadian Farm Organic Moroccan Vegetarian Meal
Serving size:	9.5 oz.	½ bag
Calories (Kcal):	300	250
Protein (gm):	18	11
Total fat (gm):	10	4
Saturated fat (gm):	1	0
Cholesterol (mg):	0	0
Dietary fiber (gm):	6	11
Sodium (mg):	630	340
Calcium (mg):	N/A	50
Iron (mg):	N/A	5

	Natural Touch Lentil Rice Loaf	Ruthie's Foods Adzuki Beans and Rice
Serving size:	1 slice	8 oz.
Calories (Kcal):	170	240
Protein (gm):	8	12
Total fat (gm):	9	< 1
Saturated fat (gm):	2.5	< 1
Cholesterol (mg):	0	0
Dietary fiber (gm):	4	5
Sodium (mg):	370	25
Calcium (mg):	20	80
Iron (mg):	1	5

	Señor Felix's Pumpkin and Mushroom Empanadas	Soy Boy Ravioli
Serving size:	1	1 cup
Calories (Kcal):	260	180
Protein (gm):	10	10
Total fat (gm):	11	3
Saturated fat (gm):	4	0.5
Cholesterol (mg):	25	0
Dietary fiber (gm):	6	N/A
Sodium (mg):	520	135
Calcium (mg):	150	80
Iron (mg):	3	2

AISLE 9

CEREALS	DINNERS
BREAKFAST	SOUP
BABY FOOD	MACROBIOTIC

TODAY'S FEATURES: WHOLE-GRAIN BREAKFAST CEREALS, INSTANT SOUP CUPS, DRIED BEAN FLAKES, AND ORGANIC CANNED BEANS

WHOLE-GRAIN BREAKFAST CEREALS

What Are They? (Why Are They Special?)

We're talking about cold breakfast cereals—the staple of everyone's cupboard. Natural breakfast cereals are worth mentioning because there's such a good variety of them—many made with unusual grains not found in the regular supermarket—most are made using *whole* grains, most are unsweetened or sweetened with fruit juices instead of refined sugar, they contain no hydrogenated fats, artificial flavorings or colorings, *and* they taste good! They also cost no more than supermarket brands.

What's more, natural breakfast cereals are not for adults only. Many brands cater to kids, with fun shapes and bold, splashy pictures on the boxes. Compared with most of the mainstream kids' cereals—loaded with sugar, hydrogenated

fats, refined flours, and artificial flavorings and colorings—
the natural cereals are more wholesome while still tasting
great and having plenty of kid appeal.

Note, too, that while we're focusing on cold cereals here,
there are lots of good hot cereal choices, too. They are a
breath of fresh air compared with mainstream brands,
because in addition to being made with whole grains (and a
wide variety of them, at that), they aren't loaded with artificial flavorings and colorings. If the oatmeal is strawberry-
flavored (or blueberry, or banana . . .) it's made with real
fruit, not synthetically flavored and colored chunks of sugar.
I'm a fan of Arrowhead Mills, Barbara's Bakery, Grain-
field's Health Valley, Kashi Company, Lifestream, and New
Morning brands, among others.

How Can I Use Them?
Eat them the usual way, but let me add that there's nothing
wrong with having a bowl of cereal for lunch, dinner, or a
snack now and then. Sometimes I have a bowl of sweetened
whole-grain breakfast cereal for dessert. I eat my cereal with
fortified vanilla soy milk.

You can make a bowl of cereal more interesting by
adding other ingredients. For instance:

- Mix two or more breakfast cereals together. I like to
  mix a small amount of granola with a whole-grain flake
  cereal or shredded wheat.

- Toss in a handful of chopped, dried fruits such as apricots, raisins, apples, pears, peaches, figs, or cherries.
  By the way, you don't have to be constipated to eat
  prunes. Chop up a handful and add them to your
  cereal—they taste great and are super-nutritious.

- Add sliced or chopped fresh fruit, especially when it's in season. Think beyond "bananas." Try chunks of cantaloupe, chopped apples or pears, blueberries, strawberries, and slivers of mango and papaya.

- Spoon a scoop of applesauce over a bowl of cereal. Add some cinnamon.

What do you pour over your cereal? Milk? If you use cow's milk, make it skim. My personal preference is vanilla soy milk, but you can use rice milk, too, or a rice/soy blend. When I was a child, my grandfather opened my eyes to the alternatives to cow's milk on cereal—he poured coffee over his. Other options: apple juice and other fruit juices. How about using carob-flavored soy milk for a chocolaty change of pace?

NUTRITIONAL FEATURES

Whole-grain cereals are a good source of dietary fiber and B vitamins, and some are substantial sources of iron, too. See how several compare in the following table:

Nutrient Composition of
Several Natural Breakfast Cereals
(Source: Manufacturer. Note that information about B vitamins is not available for these products)

	Arrowhead Mills Spelt Flakes	Barbara's Bakery High 5 Cereal
Serving size:	1 cup	¾ cup
Calories (Kcal):	100	100
Protein (gm):	5	3

Total fat (gm):	1	0.5
Saturated fat (gm):	0	0
Cholesterol (mg):	0	0
Dietary fiber (gm):	3	5
Sodium (mg):	60	180
Iron (mg):	1	1

	Grainfield's Multigrain Flakes with Rice Bran	Health Valley Organic Bran Cereal with Raisins
Serving size:	¾ cup	¾ cup
Calories (Kcal):	110	190
Protein (gm):	2	6
Total fat (gm):	0.5	0
Saturated fat (gm):	0	0
Cholesterol (mg):	0	0
Dietary fiber (gm):	2	7
Sodium (mg):	10	10
Iron (mg):	1	1

	Kashi Company Honey Puffed Kashi	Lifestream 8 Grain Flakes
Serving size:	1 cup	1 cup
Calories (Kcal):	120	210
Protein (gm):	3	6
Total fat (gm):	1	0
Saturated fat (gm):	0	0
Cholesterol (mg):	0	0
Dietary fiber (gm):	2	6
Sodium (gm):	6	20
Iron (mg):	1	3

**New Morning Cocoa Crispy
Frosted Brown Rice**

Serving size:	1 cup
Calories (Kcal):	210
Total fat (gm):	1.5
Saturated fat (gm):	0
Cholesterol (mg):	0
Dietary fiber (gm):	6
Sodium (mg):	40
Iron (mg):	1

INSTANT SOUP CUPS

What Are They?

You've probably seen these in the regular supermarket—one of the most popular brands, Fantastic Foods, started out in natural foods stores and can now be found in supermarkets everywhere. Nile Spice brand is another example. These are single-serving, cardboard cups of soup mix. Just peel back the paper lid, add boiling water, stir, and in a couple of minutes, you've got soup. There are even some varieties that combine beans or lentils and grains, such as lentils with couscous, and red beans with rice.

How Can I Use Them?

Use them at home as a convenience food for a quick meal or snack. These are light and portable, so they make a good choice for school and office, for car trips (just stop at a gas station/food mart for hot water), in a backpack, or to take to the gym for an energy boost.

To make one of my favorite quick meals at home, I bake a potato in the microwave oven—it takes only seven or eight minutes (if you don't use a microwave oven, get your baked potato going in the conventional oven ahead of time). While that's cooking, I boil some water and mix a lentil soup cup. Let the soup set for a couple of minutes until it thickens a little. When the potato is ready, slice it open on a plate and pour the soup over it, like "lentil gravy." It's a delicious combination. I usually have a mixed green salad and glass of fruit juice (or my favorite orange juice/carrot juice blend) with it. What a healthy meal, and it takes less than ten minutes to fix!

I also like to fix a black bean soup cup, let it thicken a little, and pour it over rice. It's a great way to use up leftover rice or other grains. I sometimes add some cooked vegetables on the side and eat this with a couple of slices of whole wheat toast. Nothing fancy. Just quick and easy and very nutritious.

It's best to hold your sodium intake to not more than about two thousand milligrams per day. Just one cup of soup can equal a quarter of your sodium "budget" or more. For that reason, when you eat a high-sodium food such as a bowl of soup, dilute or balance the sodium by choosing low-sodium foods for the remainder of the meal. For example, with a bowl of split-pea-and-carrot soup, you might have a mixed green salad with vinegar and oil dressing, a big chunk of Italian bread brushed with olive oil and minced garlic, and a bowl of fresh fruit salad with a sprig of mint for dessert. The soup may be high in sodium, but you've added very little more by your other food choices.

Nutritional Features

"Soup is good food," or so the saying goes. Well, the healthiest soups are those that are highest in dietary fiber, lowest in saturated fat (that leaves out a lot of regular cream soups), and lowest in sodium. Soups can be wickedly high in sodium. Most natural brand soups are high in sodium but lower than the mainstream products. Read labels and compare. Buy those with the most fiber, least saturated fat, and least sodium.

The table below shows the nutrient composition of several natural soup cups. Not only are they good sources of fiber, but some are rich in protein, vitamins A and C, calcium, and iron, too. You'll see from the table below that I'm partial to Fantastic Foods and Nile Spice brands.

Nutrient Composition of Selected Soup Cups
(8 ounces each)
(Source: Manufacturer)

	Fantastic Foods Cha-Cha Chili	Fantastic Foods Creamy Corn and Potato Chowder
Calories (Kcal):	220	170
Protein (gm):	18	7
Total fat (gm):	1	1
Saturated fat (gm):	0	0
Cholesterol (mg):	0	0
Dietary fiber (gm):	13	2
Sodium (mg):	470	580
Vitamin A (I.U.):	2,000	1,000
Vitamin C (mg):	15	20
Calcium (mg):	100	150
Iron (mg):	4.5	3

	Fantastic Foods Rice and Beans Bombay Curry	Nile Spice Couscous Garbanzo
Calories (Kcal):	230	220
Protein (gm):	12	9
Total fat (gm):	3	2.5
Saturated fat (gm):	1.5	0
Cholesterol (mg):	0	0
Dietary fiber (gm):	8	2
Sodium (mg):	470	500
Vitamin A (I.U.):	1,500	0
Vitamin C (mg):	15	4
Calcium (mg):	40	60
Iron (mg):	7	2

DRIED BEAN FLAKES AND ORGANIC CANNED BEANS

What Are They?

You know what canned beans are, but how many different kinds have you tried? Just garbanzos and red kidney beans? I thought so. Well, it's time to pick up a can of black beans, pinto beans, small white beans, black-eyed peas, white kidney beans—see what your store stocks. I've always maintained that if you have beans, pasta, and rice in your kitchen, you've got what you need to make a meal.

Organic canned beans are one of the best all-around convenience products that you'll find in the natural foods store. Another contender is dried bean flakes, which you may have to look a little harder to find. Pinto bean flakes and black bean flakes by Taste Adventure may be hiding among the soup cups and canned soups. They come in one-pint or one-quart cardboard boxes that look like milk cartons. Ask the store manager for help if you can't find them. These are a "must have." Buy both.

Another brand of bean flakes you may see is Fantastic Foods. This company makes both pinto bean and black bean flakes as well. They are packaged in boxes that you may find on the shelf near the dry mixes such as vegetarian chili mix or grain mixes. You may find dried bean flakes in the bulk bins, too.

How Can I Use Them?

Dried bean flakes give you smooth, creamy bean dip or spread in only five minutes. When I'm not in the mood to mash canned beans by hand to make burrito or taco filling, I mix up some bean flakes instead. I like to alternate between pinto bean flakes and black bean flakes for making taco and burrito fillings. Black beans are an especially striking color contrast to the diced red tomatoes, white and green minced scallions, chopped greens, and salsa that I usually add to my Mexican-style foods.

• BLACK BEAN BURRITOS •

Large flour tortilla
½ cup black bean flakes, prepared according to package instructions (this step takes about five minutes once you have boiled the water)
Small ripe tomato, diced
One green onion, sliced thinly
Several spinach leaves, chopped
3 tablespoons salsa
2 tablespoons plain soy yogurt

Lay the tortilla flat on a dinner plate. Spoon the black beans onto the tortilla, then sprinkle tomato, onion, and spinach evenly over the beans. Add salsa. Roll the tortilla up jelly roll–

style. Place a large dollop of soy yogurt on top. Makes 1 large burrito. Alternative: in a similar fashion, fill 2 taco shells.

Nutritional content (one burrito): Calories (Kcal): 275, Protein (gm): 14, Total fat (gm): 4.5 Saturated fat (gm): 0, Cholesterol (mg): 0, Dietary fiber (gm): 6, Sodium (mg): 197, Calcium (mg): 108, Iron (mg): 4, Zinc (mg): 1

There seems to be almost an infinite number of ways to use canned beans, with a multitude of variations, considering all of the different kinds of beans available. Some of my favorite ways to serve canned beans follow. In examples where the beans are mashed, you can substitute rehydrated bean flakes to save time.

- Black beans over yellow saffron rice

- Black-eyed peas and rice (in the South, it's called Hoppin' John)

- Many-bean chili (I like to use garbanzo, pinto, and red kidney beans and throw in a handful of corn for color)

- Hummus (garbanzo bean spread)

- Mashed pinto beans (mixed with onion and garlic powders) as filling for regular or soft tacos, burritos, and on top of nachos

- Black bean dip served with cilantro and toasted pita bread wedges, vegetable sticks, or large tortilla chips

- A plain bowl of warm black beans topped with a dollop of salsa

- Black bean soup

- Navy bean soup

- Beans with stewed tomatoes and vegetables over rice

- Bean chili served over brown rice

- Four-bean salad (made with garbanzo beans, red kidney beans, green, and wax beans)

- Garbanzo beans on a mixed green salad

- White kidney beans tossed with pasta and garlic

- Beans on toast

Nutritional Features

I'd be hard-pressed to name a food that's a better source of dietary fiber than dried beans and peas (legumes). Canned beans and dry bean flakes are a rich source of soluble fiber. That's the kind of fiber that helps to lower your blood cholesterol level (the same type found in oat bran and oatmeal), as well as helping to control blood sugar levels.

Current dietary recommendations call for a minimum dietary fiber intake of thirty-five grams per day and preferably more. Just one cup of pinto beans or black beans contains seven grams of fiber. A good-sized helping of bean chili or bean soup could give you as much as fourteen grams of fiber, or almost half of your minimum daily goal. Beans are also rich in protein, vitamins, and minerals, including iron and zinc.

Nutrient Content of 1 Cup of Organic Beans

(Source: Manufacturer, Westbrae Natural;
note information about zinc is not available)

	Black	Kidney	Garbanzo	Pinto	Red
Calories (Kcal):	180	180	220	180	180
Protein (gm):	12	12	12	10	12
Total fat (gm):	0	0	4	0	0
Saturated fat (gm):	0	0	0	0	0
Cholesterol (mg):	0	0	0	0	0
Dietary fiber (gm):	8	8	10	12	8
Sodium (gm):	220	220	220	220	220
Calcium (mg):	40	40	40	40	40
Iron (mg):	3	3	2	3	3

• EASY HUMMUS •

Hummus is a traditional Middle Eastern bean dip made from garbanzo beans (also known as chickpeas). It's delicious served cold as a dip for carrot sticks or as a sandwich filling (add some alfalfa sprouts and grated carrots). Traditionally, it's served warm in a shallow dish with a squeeze of fresh lemon juice and a drizzle of olive oil on top. Wedges of pita bread are used to scoop the dip.

This recipe is a snap to make. Serve it warm or cold. It will keep in the refrigerator for one week.

2 15-ounce cans of garbanzo beans (no need to drain, unless you want a thicker dip or if you want to rinse the beans to remove the salt)
2 teaspoons of minced garlic

4 tablespoons of tahini (sesame seed paste; optional: substitute 2 tablespoons olive oil for 2 tablespoons of tahini)
Juice from one freshly squeezed lemon (or to taste)
¼ teaspoon white pepper
Fresh lemon wedges, small sweet pickles, olive oil, and paprika garnish

Place first 5 ingredients in a blender or food processor and blend until smooth and creamy. If using drained garbanzo beans, add a small amount of water or additional lemon juice to facilitate blending as needed.

Serve in a shallow dish or on a plate. Garnish with small, thin wedges of lemon, black olives, and/or tiny strips of pickle arranged around the edge of the dish or plate. Swirl a small amount of olive oil on top and sprinkle with paprika. Serve with pita bread wedges that have been brushed with olive oil and garlic and lightly toasted in the oven.

Yield: About 4 half-cup servings.

Nutrient content per serving: Calories (Kcal): 262, Protein (gm): 12, Total fat (gm): 8, Saturated fat (gm): 0, Cholesterol (mg): 0, Dietary fiber (gm): 10.5, Sodium (mg): 850 (dip is low in sodium if canned beans are rinsed), Calcium (mg): 99, Iron (mg): 6, Zinc (mg): 3

AISLE 10

COOKIES	CANDY
CRACKERS	SNACKS
RICE CAKES	CHIPS
TEAS	DIPS

TODAY'S FEATURES: WHOLE-GRAIN COOKIES AND CRACKERS; CHIPS AND SNACKS

WHOLE-GRAIN COOKIES AND CRACKERS

What Are They? (Why Are They Special?)

I'm pointing these products out because they have several important advantages over mainstream brands, and people who aren't familiar with natural foods stores generally don't know that they exist.

Most mainstream cookies are nothing more than refined flour, hydrogenated fat, sugar, and artificial flavorings. The crackers? Refined flour, hydrogenated fat, and salt. As for the proliferation of fat-free cookies and crackers, they're essentially the same ingredients minus the fat, plus gums and additional conditioners. Some have extra sugar to make up for the flavor the fat would have provided. Consequently, most of the mainstream fat-free cookies and crackers are either syrupy sweet or they taste like cardboard, in my humble opinion.

In contrast, natural cookies and crackers are generally made with whole grains and contain no hydrogenated fats. Most use little, if any, refined sweeteners; many are sweetened with fruit juice. The sodium content is often lower than in mainstream brands, and there are no artificial flavorings or colorings or other synthetic additives. In my view, that makes them more wholesome than mainstream cookies and crackers, particularly when you choose those made with whole grains rather than refined flour.

How Can I Use Them?

Let's say it's midnight and you'd like nothing better than a plateful of cookies and a big glass of soy milk. Nothing wrong with that, especially if the cookies are made with whole-grain flour and other wholesome ingredients.

Cookies and crackers are examples of foods that fill in the gaps in our diets—they're dessert or a snack or an appetizer. They're supplemental. Even in the case of natural brands, they aren't necessarily "great" for you. But unlike most mainstream products, natural products are likely to be "nutritional neutrals" at worst—they're not going to help you, but they won't hurt you either. Considering the big role these foods play in the lives of many of us, I think it's worth seeking out the healthiest choices.

So when your kids want an after-school snack, or you want something to munch on while you're working late, natural cookies and crackers are generally a better choice than most mainstream brands.

When you sample natural cookies and crackers, try several different brands and varieties of the same brand. There are lots of products out there. There is also substantial variation in flavor and texture among products. I've found some taste like plywood, while others are great. One of my favorite brands is Barbara's Bakery. You may find that you prefer products made with one type of sweetener over another. For instance, I've never liked cookies flavored with fruit juice, but I love many that are sweetened with other forms of sugar. Remember: when you experiment with new foods, you're bound to stumble upon a dud now and then, but you'll also find new favorites.

Nutritional Features

Most natural cookies and crackers aren't nutritional power-houses, but they're healthier than most mainstream brands. They can range from being "nutritional neutrals" to being fairly good sources of dietary fiber and some B vitamins. What they *don't* contain matters, too (no hydrogenated fats, no artificial flavorings, and so on).

Nutritional Composition of Selected Natural Cookies

(Source: Manufacturer. Note: information about B vitamin content is not available)

	Barbara's Bakery Fat-Free Double Chocolate Mini Cookies	Health Valley Original Amaranth Graham Crackers
Serving size:	6 cookies	6 crackers
Calories (Kcal):	100	120
Protein (gm):	2	3
Total fat (gm):	0	3
Saturated fat (gm):	0	0
Cholesterol (mg):	0	0
Dietary fiber (gm):	1	3
Sodium (mg):	135	80
Calcium (mg):	20	40
Iron (mg):	1	1

	Marin Brand Fig Bars	Tree of Life Mint Creme Supremes
Serving size:	2 fig bars	2 cookies
Calories (Kcal):	120	120
Protein (gm):	2	1
Total fat (gm):	3	5
Saturated fat (gm):	1	0
Cholesterol (mg):	0	0
Dietary fiber (gm):	3	1
Sodium (mg):	100	90
Calcium (mg):	20	20
Iron (mg):	40	0.5

Nutritional Composition of Selected Natural Crackers

(Source: Manufacturer. Note: information is not
available for B vitamins)

	Hain Stone Ground Organic Whole Wheat Crackers	Health Valley Fat-Free Vegetable Crackers
Serving size:	11 crackers	6
Calories (Kcal):	130	50
Protein (gm):	3	2
Total fat (gm):	6	0
Saturated fat (gm):	0	0
Cholesterol (mg):	0	0
Dietary fiber (gm):	1	2
Sodium (mg):	135	80
Calcium (mg):	0	20
Iron (mg):	1	20

	Lifestream Sesame Seed Crackers	Tree of Life Saltine Crackers
Serving size:	8	4
Calories (Kcal):	84	50
Protein (gm):	2.5	2
Total fat (gm):	2	0
Saturated fat (gm):	N/A	0
Cholesterol (mg):	N/A	0
Dietary fiber (gm):	2.5	0
Sodium (mg):	116	140
Calcium (mg):	N/A	0
Iron (mg):	60	40

CHIPS AND SNACKS

What Are They? (Why Are They Special?)
Question: What's more American than apple pie?
Answer: Chips. All kinds of them.

Potato chips, corn chips, and tortilla chips. Ranch flavor, nacho cheese flavor, barbecue, and sour cream and chives. Chips and similar snacks are ubiquitous in our culture. Order a sandwich at a restaurant and you're likely to get chips on the side. A party without a big bowl of chips and dip? It wouldn't be a party, would it?

Mainstream chips and snacks are typically salty, greasy, empty-calorie foods. Some are artificially flavored and colored. Most contain hydrogenated oils. Their natural counterparts aren't nutritional powerhouses, but they're "the best of the worst." Some are made with whole grains, some are lower in sodium than the mainstream brands, some are fat-free (as are some mainstream brands now), and all of them are naturally flavored and colored.

If you want chips and similar snack foods, natural products are the more wholesome choice. You may have seen one or two natural brands at your neighborhood supermarket, but most people don't realize how many more choices are available in natural foods stores. That's why I'm pointing them out.

• LIGHT AND SPICY CRACKER AND CHIP DIP •

This light dip can be eaten with raw vegetable sticks, potato or vegetable chips, and crackers. I eat leftover dip on top of baked potatoes. The dip will keep in the refrigerator, covered, for one to two weeks.

1 cup plain soy yogurt
¼ cup minced onion
¼ teaspoon salt
1 teaspoon chili powder
½ teaspoon garlic powder
½ teaspoon cumin

In a small bowl, whisk all ingredients together thoroughly. Chill for at least 2 hours before serving.

Makes about 1¼ cups of dip.

Nutritional content per two-tablespoon serving: Calories (Kcal): 20, Protein (gm): 1, Total fat (gm): 1, Saturated fat (gm): 0, Cholesterol (mg): 0, Dietary fiber (gm): 0, Sodium (mg): 60, Calcium (mg): 7, Iron (mg) 0, Zinc (mg): 0

How Can I Use Them?

Chips and similar snack foods don't provide much in the way of nutrition. They're filler foods; finger foods—foods that we like to munch on because they taste good, they're convenient, and we associate them with fun.

That's fine, as long as foods like these don't displace too much of the good stuff—the fruits, vegetables, and whole grains that should make up the backbone of a health-supporting diet. And if you're going to indulge in chips and such, you might as well choose those that are the most nutritious and least detrimental to your health. Usually, that means choosing natural products.

To flavor popcorn without adding sodium and saturated fat, spritz hot popcorn lightly with olive oil from a small plant mister or pump spray (some grocery stores carry one such product, called "Misto"). Then sprinkle the popcorn with chili powder, cayenne pepper, garlic powder, or any other favorite herb or spice mixture, and toss well.

Nutritional Features

Natural snack chips vary in fat content, although none of the fat is hydrogenated and little, if any, is saturated. Most provide a couple of grams of protein and dietary fiber in every ounce and small amounts of vitamins and minerals. When I indulge in them, I prefer Barbara's, Bearitos, Garden of Eatin', Guiltless Gourmet, and Terra brands.

Nutrient Content of
One Ounce of Natural Snack Chips
(Source: Manufacturer)

	Barbara's Pinto Chips	Bearitos Blue Corn Tortilla Chips
Calories (Kcal):	130	140
Protein (gm):	2	2
Total fat (gm):	6	7
Saturated fat (gm):	1	1
Cholesterol (mg):	0	0
Dietary fiber (gm):	2	2
Sodium (mg):	210	120
Calcium (mg):	40	40
Iron (mg):	trace	trace

	Garden of Eatin' Black Bean Chili Chips	Guiltless Gourmet Baked Not Fried Potato Chips, Lightly Salted
Calories (Kcal):	140	110
Protein (gm):	2	2
Total fat (gm):	7	1.5
Saturated fat (gm):	0.5	0
Cholesterol (mg):	0	0
Dietary fiber (gm):	2	1
Sodium (mg):	90	180
Calcium (mg):	40	20
Iron (mg):	1	trace

**Terra Vegetable Chips,
Cinnamon Spiced Sweet Potato**

Calories (Kcal):	140
Protein (gm):	1
Total fat (gm):	7
Saturated fat (gm):	1
Cholesterol (mg):	0
Dietary fiber (gm):	2
Sodium (mg):	30
Calcium (mg):	40
Iron (mg):	1

AISLE 11

BREAD	BEER
PITA	DRINKS
BAGELS	TAKEOUT
FROZEN BARS	WATER

TODAY'S FEATURE: WHOLE-GRAIN BREADS, INCLUDING WHOLE-GRAIN SPECIALTY BREADS

What Is It? (Why Is It Special?)

Heavy, coarse-grained, flavorful bread made from organic whole grains. Short ingredient lists. No synthetic preservatives, artificial flavorings or colorings. No hydrogenated fats. This type of bread is easy to find at the natural foods store. It's the most nutritious bread you can buy, and once you've eaten it, there's no going back.

If you've never tried natural, whole-grain breads, you don't know what you're missing. Standard supermarket varieties pale in comparison. This is like the difference between drinking orange juice made from frozen concentrate or enjoying freshly squeezed orange juice. The former may taste good, but the experience of drinking the latter is on a whole other level. Natural, whole-grain breads are premium-quality food. I like Matthews, Rudolph's, and Shiloh Farms brand breads, among others.

How Can I Use It?

Good quality, whole-grain breads make everything you make with them taste better. I love to use natural, whole-grain breads for French toast *(see recipe below)* and bread pudding. I crumble them and use them in vegetable casseroles. And they're unsurpassed for making plain ol' cinnamon toast.

• HEALTHY FRENCH TOAST •

2 large, ripe bananas
1 cup plain or vanilla soy milk (I use Eden Soy Extra Vanilla)
¼ teaspoon nutmeg
½ teaspoon vanilla
8 slices multigrain bread
Powdered sugar (optional)

In a blender or food processor, blend the bananas, soy milk, nutmeg, and vanilla until smooth. Pour the mixture into a pie pan or similar large, flat dish.

Heat a lightly oiled griddle (it's hot enough when a drop of water spatters when dripped onto the griddle). Dip both sides of the bread into the mixture and cook until browned on each side.

Dust each piece of French toast with a sprinkling of powdered sugar (optional). Serve with warm maple syrup.

Serves 4.

Nutritional content per serving: Calories (Kcal): 245, Total fat (gm): 3, Saturated fat (gm): 0, Cholesterol (mg): 0, Protein (gm):

7, Dietary fiber (gm): 4.5, Sodium (mg): 229, Calcium (mg): 97,
Iron (mg): 2, Zinc (mg): 1

When you choose bread, the most important features
include the presence of whole grains and the absence of
hydrogenated fats or other added saturated fats. Don't
worry as much about the calorie content. "Light" and "thin-
sliced" breads are marketed by some mainstream companies for their lower calorie content, playing on the myth that
bread is fattening. While calories do count at some level,
bread is not a particularly fattening food, relatively speaking. The only reason to buy thinly sliced bread is if you just
happen to prefer it that way.

Nutritional Features

Natural, whole-grain breads are a good source of protein, B
vitamins, and dietary fiber. Some are good sources of iron
and zinc.

Nutrient Content of One Slice of Natural, Whole-Grain Bread

(Source: Manufacturer.
Note: information not available for zinc content)

	Berlin Natural Bakery Sprouted Seed Bread	Matthews All Natural 100% Whole Wheat Bread
Calories (Kcal):	80	80
Protein (gm):	4	3
Total fat (gm):	0.5	1.5
Saturated fat (gm):	0	0
Cholesterol (mg):	0	0

Dietary fiber (gm):	2	2
Sodium (mg):	140	160
Calcium (mg):	0	0
Iron (mg):	1	1

	Rudolph's 100% Rye with Sunflower Seed	**Rudolph's Salt-Free 100% Rye**
Calories (Kcal):	140	140
Protein (gm):	6	5
Total fat (gm):	3	0
Saturated fat (gm):	0	0
Cholesterol (mg):	0	0
Dietary fiber (gm):	6	6
Sodium (mg):	0	0
Calcium (mg):	0	N/A
Iron (mg):	0	N/A

	Shiloh Farms Sprouted Five Grain Bread
Calories (Kcal):	90
Protein (gm):	5
Total fat (gm):	5
Saturated fat (gm):	0
Cholesterol (mg):	0
Dietary fiber (gm):	4
Sodium (mg):	110
Calcium (mg):	N/A
Iron (mg):	2

Buying and Storing Whole-Grain Bread

Natural breads don't keep as long as breads that contain additives to prolong shelf life. For that reason, I usually put my loaves in the refrigerator within a day or two of purchase. They should be stored in a plastic bag or other airtight container to keep them from drying out too quickly. Week-old bread that is becoming dry can be toasted or used to make French toast or bread pudding. You can also brush it with olive oil, sprinkle on a bit of garlic powder or an herb mixture, and toast it in the oven. Break it apart and use it as croutons on salads or in soup.

• SIMPLE APPLE BREAD PUDDING •

When I make this recipe, I love to use raisin walnut whole wheat bread or sunflower wheat bread, but any whole-grain bread works well.

4 slices of whole-grain bread cut into cubes
1½ cups organic applesauce
¼ teaspoon ground cinnamon, plus additional for dusting
Dash of ground nutmeg
2 tablespoons of vegetable oil
2 cups of fortified soy milk
Vegetarian egg replacer equivalent to 2 whole eggs
½ cup sugar
1 teaspoon vanilla
Dash of salt

Oil an 8 × 8-inch baking dish. Spread half of the bread cubes on the bottom of the dish. Combine applesauce, cinnamon, and nutmeg. Spread this mixture over the bread cubes. Layer the remaining bread cubes over the top of applesauce mixture and brush with vegetable oil.

Combine soy milk, egg replacer, sugar, vanilla, and salt. Pour over contents of dish. Dust the top with cinnamon. Bake, uncovered, at 350 degrees F until a knife inserted into the pudding comes out clean—about 1 hour.

Yield: 6 servings.

Nutrient content per serving: Calories (Kcal): 226, Protein (gm): 4, Total fat (gm): 7, Saturated fat (gm): 1, Cholesterol (mg): 0, Dietary fiber (gm): 3, Sodium (mg): 180, Calcium (mg): 78, Iron (mg): 1

WHOLE-GRAIN SPECIALTY BREADS

What Are They?

For me, fresh, whole-grain bakery breads are my greatest treat at the natural foods store. Most of them are made at local bakeries. Because they contain no artificial preservatives, they keep only for a few days on the shelves. At my neighborhood natural foods store, they don't even keep *that* long—they fly off the shelves.

I described commercial, natural whole-grain breads at the beginning of this chapter, but bakery breads are unique. They are usually fresher, they are made in a greater variety of shapes (big, round loaves; small, squat loaves; long, narrow baguettes; dinner rolls; buns), and they come in a range of interesting and often unusual flavors and blends of ingredients.

How Can I Use Them?

My natural foods store carries natural breads made with organic flours, made fresh at a bakery right next door. My favorite is a heavy, coarse-grained raisin walnut bread. I like to make French toast and peanut-butter-and-banana sandwiches with it, and I eat it toasted for breakfast instead of eating a doughnut or pastry. It's so good that sometimes I have a slice or two for dessert.

I also like whole wheat lavosh bread. It's a type of unleavened Middle Eastern bread—a big, round, flat "loaf" that resembles a giant flour tortilla. One of my favorite meals is made by spreading a filling—usually refried pinto beans or black beans—over the lavosh, adding chopped lettuce (and cilantro, if you like it), tomatoes, onions, and salsa, rolling it up jelly roll–style, then slicing the roll into two- or three-inch pieces. These can be arranged on a platter on their sides, like pinwheels; they're colorful and festive.

I like to buy whole wheat burger rolls for my veggie burgers as well as for making tempeh sloppy joe's. The bakery rolls seem to have a better texture and taste fresher to me than the commercial rolls. I like to keep a variety of interesting types of breads on hand. I alternate between various types of fresh bagels and rolls, sunflower seed bread, sprouted wheat bread, multigrain breads, fruited breads, oatmeal bread, and plain old whole wheat bread. A sandwich filling such as hummus can take on different personalities depending upon whether it's served in a pita pocket, on a bagel, or on a slice of toast.

Nutritional Features
See page 167.

Buying and Storing Whole-Grain Specialty Breads
Bakery breads will keep longer if you store them in the refrigerator. If a loaf is large and I think that it'll dry out in the refrigerator before I can eat it all, I sometimes place half in a freezer bag or other airtight container and store it in the freezer. Many people, however, prefer the taste and texture of fresh bread that has never been frozen or refrigerated. In that case, you'll need to keep the bread in a breadbox or airtight plastic bag and eat it before it spoils, which may be a week or less.

AISLE 12

BAKERY   **DELI**

TODAY'S FEATURES:
READY-MADE SALADS AND SPREADS

READY-MADE SALADS AND SPREADS

What Are They?

Natural foods stores often have their own café, where you can order a meal prepared with natural ingredients. This is a great way to sample dishes you've never tried before, especially some of the ethnic dishes that are made with unfamiliar ingredients. If you've been planning to try a new and unusual recipe at home, it helps to taste it at the store first so that you'll know what you're aiming for when you make it yourself.

In addition to the café, many stores also have deli counters, where they sell portions of the entrées served in the café as well as salads, appetizers, dips and spreads, and desserts. Sometimes single servings of these foods are sold in a refrigerator case in the store as well.

Salads and spreads are a good place to start when you are experimenting with new foods. They're almost universally liked, and they're usually simple enough to make at home after you've tried them ready-made. They're also versatile. Spreads can be used as dips for vegetables and crackers as well as for sandwich fillings. Salads can be a meal in themselves, a convenient side dish, or an addition to a pita pocket sandwich.

Some popular salads and spreads include:

- Hummus—a blended Middle Eastern chickpea spread, it can be made in a variety of flavors, including lemon, garlic, dill, roasted red pepper, scallions, mixed spices, vegetable, black olive, and many others *(see recipe on page 152)*.

- Baba ganoujh—a Middle Eastern dip or spread made with eggplant, garlic, and tahini.

- Tofu salad (or mock egg salad; *see recipe on page 85)*.

- Tabouli—a Middle Eastern salad made with bulgur wheat and minced vegetables and mint *(see recipe on pages 176)*.

- Lentil-and-brown rice salad *(see recipe on page 177)*.

- Fruited wheat berry salad.

- Fruited couscous salad—small pieces of fruit tossed with couscous, which is a Middle Eastern grain dish made of tiny bits of semolina. Cooked couscous resembles corn grits, only bigger.

Notice that many of the above are of Middle Eastern origin. There are many, many other salads and spreads that you'll want to try. Stores vary in their offerings. You may find hummus made with black beans instead of chickpeas.

You'll see dips made from pureed peas with garlic or other spices added. You'll find numerous grain-based salads, as well as salads made with unfamiliar vegetables such as jicama and arugula. Now's your chance to explore the world without leaving your zip code.

How Can I Use Them?

Well, you're really limited only by your imagination. You can use spreads such as black bean hummus, chickpea hummus, and baba ganoujh as an appetizer served with wedges of pita bread or vegetable pieces for dipping. You can spread them inside a pita pocket and add a scoop of tabouli or some grated carrots. I like to spread hummus on a whole wheat flour tortilla and roll it up for a burrito-style sandwich. Sometimes I add tabouli, chopped spinach and tomatoes, or finely minced cucumber salad.

Salads don't have to be side dishes. Use tabouli, tofu salad, couscous, or wheat berry salad as fillings for tomato halves or a wedge of cantaloupe. Serve a large portion of a salad as an entrée and have a cup of hot soup and a slice of good bread along with it.

....

While you're in the deli area, sample the fresh salsa. There are many variations of the standard, including salsa with cilantro, raspberry salsa, pineapple salsa, and mixtures of salsa with vegetables such as corn and black beans. These are great for topping baked potatoes, pieces of flat bread, and salads, and some of the more unique flavors can add a new twist to your usual bean burrito, bean taco, or nachos. Also try fresh marinara sauce if it's available. You can use it on pasta, spaghetti squash, and for pizza topping.

....

Nutritional Features

Many of the ready-made salads and spreads described here are made with olive oil, and some contain tahini. These foods can range from low to moderate in fat content. If weight is an issue for you, you may need to use these foods infrequently, in small portions, or balance them with lower-calorie fruits and vegetables. If you are not unduly concerned about weight, then the primarily monounsaturated fats used to make these foods are not a problem.

In general, the foods I've described are rich in dietary fiber and are good sources of protein, vitamins, and minerals. They are low in saturated fat and are cholesterol-free. They vary widely in nutritional composition, depending upon the recipes used.

• SIMPLE TABOULI •

Tabouli is a cold, grain-based salad of Middle Eastern origin. Serve it as a side dish alongside a falafel sandwich or as a side salad on a lettuce leaf. I like to add a spoonful to pita pocket sandwiches—the lemon juice and mint adds a lot of zip.

2 cups water
1 cup bulgur wheat
2 medium, ripe tomatoes, chopped finely
3–4 scallions (white and green parts), chopped finely
½ of a medium cucumber, peeled, and chopped finely
¼ cup chopped parsley
2 tablespoons chopped fresh mint
2 tablespoons olive oil
Juice of 2 fresh lemons
Salt and pepper to taste (optional)

Heat the water (with salt, if desired) in a saucepan until it is boiling, then add the bulgur wheat. Stir, turn off the heat, and cover the pan tightly with a lid. Set the pan aside and let the bulgur soak for 1–2 hours, until the water has been absorbed. Let the bulgur cool. Once it has cooled, drain off any excess water, using a strainer, if necessary. Add the remaining ingredients and toss well.

Yield: 6 servings.

Nutrient content per serving: Calories (Kcal): 160, Protein (gm): 3, Total fat (gm): 5, Saturated fat (gm): <1, Cholesterol (mg): 0, Dietary fiber (gm): 6, Sodium (mg): 6 or more if salt is added, Calcium (mg): 23, Iron (mg): 2, Vitamin A (I.U.): 853, Vitamin C (mg): 18

Buying and Storing Salads and Spreads
Most fresh salads only keep for a few days in the refrigerator before they begin to spoil. Buy only what you can reasonably eat in two or three days. Spreads usually keep a little longer—up to a week is a good bet. If you keep them tightly covered, some (such as hummus) will keep for two weeks in the refrigerator.

• BROWN-RICE-AND-LENTIL VINAIGRETTE SALAD •

1 cup cooked brown rice
1 cup cooked lentils
¼ cup finely minced carrot
¼ cup minced cucumber
¼ cup chopped green onion
¼ cup finely chopped green pepper

DRESSING

2 tablespoons olive oil
1 tablespoon red wine vinegar
1 tablespoon lemon juice
½ teaspoon salt

Combine brown rice, lentils, and vegetables and toss together in a mixing bowl. For the dressing, combine oil, vinegar, lemon juice, and salt in a small cup. Pour dressing over salad and toss well. Chill for at least 2 hours before serving.

Makes 6 half-cup servings.

Nutritional content per serving: Calories (Kcal): 110, Protein (gm): 3.5, Total fat (gm): 5, Saturated fat (gm): 1, Cholesterol (mg): 0, Dietary fiber (gm): 2, Sodium (mg): 190, Calcium (mg): 16, Iron (mg): 1, Zinc (mg): 0

YOU MAY ALSO BE
INTERESTED IN . . .

OTHER RESOURCES

If you have an interest in natural foods, then you might find some of these additional resources helpful. The list is a sampling of organizations, agencies, magazines and newsletters, books and cookbooks that pertain to the natural products industry. Those resources that I've chosen to include are oriented toward helping consumers understand the regulations that apply to the natural products industry, the science of nutrition and health, or ways to incorporate more natural foods into their lifestyles. The list is not exhaustive, but it's a good starting point for anyone wanting to learn more about natural foods and their role in maintaining a health-supporting diet and lifestyle.

ORGANIZATIONS

The American Botanical Council
  (see Aisle 6, page 107)

The American Dietetic Association
216 West Jackson Blvd., Suite 800
Chicago, IL 60606-6995

Phone: 312-899-0040
Toll-free consumer nutrition hotline: 800-366-1655
Web site: http://www.eatright.org

The American Dietetic Association (ADA) is the largest membership organization of dietetics professionals. Within the Association is a specialty group for dietitians who are interested in plant-based, or vegetarian, diets. The Vegetarian Nutrition Dietetic Practice Group (VN DPG) publishes a quarterly newsletter, *Issues in Vegetarian Dietetics,* that is available by subscription to non-members. Call the Association's Division of Practice at the main number above for more information. The VN DPG also produces consumer materials that are available for purchase, and at the time of writing is setting up a Web site for consumers and professionals through which they can access materials and information about vegetarian diets.

Another ADA practice group, Environmental Nutrition (EN), is devoted to issues concerning food and the environment. Information about materials available for consumers can be obtained by phoning the ADA's Division of Practice at the main number above.

The ADA also has a toll-free consumer hotline available (number above) through which consumers can speak with a registered dietitian about any nutrition-related matter or request a referral to a nutritionist in their local area specializing in vegetarian nutrition, natural foods or alternative care, or any other area of practice. The hotline also runs monthly recorded nutrition messages. Spanish language options are also available.

The ADA's National Center for Nutrition and Dietetics (NCND) is the Association's public education arm, and it can be reached at the toll-free number above. The NCND has materials that can be sent free of charge to consumers upon request. For instance, callers can request a copy of the ADA's position paper on vegetarian diets or a copy of the Association's brochure *Eating Well—the Vegetarian Way.*

The Center for Science in the Public Interest
1875 Connecticut Avenue, NW, Suite 300
Washington, DC 20009
Phone: 202-332-9110
Web site: http://www.cspinet.org

The Center for Science in the Public Interest (CSPI) is a non-profit health advocacy group that educates consumers and professionals and advocates for governmental and corporate policy changes. The focus of the group's work is health and nutrition policy. The Center publishes the newsletter *Nutrition Action Health Letter* (ten issues per year).

Committee for Sustainable Agriculture
406 Main Street, Suite 313
Watsonville, CA 95076
Phone: 408-763-2111

The Committee for Sustainable Agriculture is a source of information for consumers (as well as farmers and retailers) about organic farming and sustainable agricultural practices.

Food Studies Institute
60 Cayuga Street
Trumansburg, NY 14886
Phone: 607-387-6884
E-mail: ad14@cornell.edu

The Food Studies Institute seeks to improve the long-term health and education of elementary-school children through a unique curriculum integrating academic disciplines with food, nutrition, culture, and the arts. The curriculum is a research-based program modeled after the award-winning Trumansburg, New York, study *Food Education in the Elementary Classroom*. The study was the doctoral thesis of Dr. Antonia Demas and was published by Cornell University in 1995.

The study demonstrated that a food-based curriculum results in a dramatic dietary acceptance of diverse healthful foods among children in the school lunch program. The study also showed that a hands-on, experiential food-based curriculum provides academic enrichment for all students. The goal of the Food Studies Institute is to replicate this program across the country, with special emphasis on schools with at-risk youth.

Mothers & Others for a Livable Planet
40 West 20th Street, 9th Floor
New York, NY 10011
Phone: 212-242-0010 or 888-ECO-INFO
Web site: http://www.mothers.org/mothers

Mothers & Others is a nonprofit educational organization working to promote ecologically sustainable food choices through its Shopper's Campaign and educational materials, including a number of publications. The group publishes the newsletter *The Green Guide to Everyday Life* (fifteen issues per year).

Oldways Preservation & Exchange Trust
25 First Street
Cambridge, MA 02141
Phone: 617-621-3000

Oldways is a nonprofit organization devoted to preserving traditions and fostering cultural exchange in food, cooking, and agriculture. One of its projects is the Chefs Collaborative 2000, a nationwide network of chefs and restaurant owners nationwide who work toward increasing industry and consumer awareness and appreciation for sustainable food choices.

The Physicians Committee for Responsible Medicine
5100 Wisconsin Avenue, NW, Suite 404
Washington, DC 20016
Phone: 202-686-2210
Web site: http://www.pcrm.org

The Physicians Committee for Responsible Medicine (PCRM) is a nonprofit organization that promotes nutrition, preventive medicine, ethical research practices, and compassionate medical policy. The group publishes the quarterly newsletter *Good Medicine*.

Public Voice for Food and Health Policy
1101 14th Street, NW, Suite 710
Washington, DC 20005
Phone: 202-371-1840
Web site: http://www.publicvoice.org/pvoice.html

Public Voice for Food and Health Policy is an advocacy organization that educates the public through media outreach about its efforts to bring about policy changes that pertain to food and health. The group has recently been involved in efforts to improve the healthfulness of school meals by advocating for regulation changes in the national school meals programs. The group is also involved in issues relating to pesticides in the food supply and sustainable agriculture.

The Vegetarian Resource Group
P.O. Box 1463
Baltimore, MD 21203
Phone: 410-366-8343 or 410-366-VEGE
Web site: http://www.vrg.org

The Vegetarian Resource Group (VRG) is a nonprofit organization that educates the public about vegetarianism and the interrelated issues of health, nutrition, ecology, ethics, and world hunger. The group publishes the bimonthly *Vegetarian Journal* (ISBN 0885-7636) and provides numerous other printed consumer education materials at a modest cost or free of charge. All health and nutrition materials are peer-reviewed by a team of medical doctors and/or registered dietitians. The group is also active in advocating for health and food policy changes in the best interests of consumers.

FEDERAL AGENCIES

The National Organic Program
U.S. Department of Agriculture
Room 2510-S, South Building
P.O. Box 96456

Washington, DC 20090-6456
Phone: 202-720-3252

The Department of Agriculture's National Organic Program (NOP) can provide information about alternative agricultural practices as well as the status of proposed federal standards for organic foods, the establishment of which the NOP oversees. You can also access copies of the *Federal Register* on the Internet to stay abreast of legislative changes concerning organic food standards.

The *Federal Register* is published Monday through Friday and is the organ through which the government publicizes regulations and legal notices issued by federal agencies, including proposed and final rules and notices of meetings such as the National Institutes of Health Advisory Committee, among others, as well as announcements of grant availability and other items of interest. View the *Federal Register* at the Superintendent of Documents home page at http://www.access.gpo.gov/su_docs/

MAGAZINES AND NEWSLETTERS

Delicious! **magazine**
Delicious! is a monthly natural foods magazine for consumers. It's available at all natural foods stores.
www.delicious-online.com

Environmental Nutrition Newsletter
52 Riverside Drive, Suite 15-A
New York, NY 10024-6599
Phone: 212-362-2066
Subscriptions: 800-829-5384
E-mail: envnutr@compuserve.com

Environmental Nutrition is published monthly and is a progressive source of information about food, nutrition, and health for consumers and health professionals.

HerbalGram

HerbalGram is a magazine published quarterly by the American Botanical Council and sold at newsstands and by subscription. (*See Aisle 6, page 107.*)

Natural Health
17 Station Street
Brookline Village, MA 02146
Phone: 617-232-1000

Natural Health (formerly *EastWest Journal*) is a monthly magazine available on newsstands or by subscription. It focuses on nutrition and environmental issues related to health as well as on alternative health topics.

Nutrition Action Healthletter
   (see Center for Science in the Public Interest)

Vegetarian Journal
   (see Vegetarian Resource Group)

Vegetarian Times
P.O. Box 570
Oak Park, IL 60303
Phone: 708-848-8100
Subscriptions: 800-829-3340
Web site: http://www.vegetariantimes.com

Vegetarian Times is a monthly magazine available on newsstands or by subscription. The magazine addresses issues related to vegetarianism, nutrition, health, the environment, animal rights, and alternative medicine. The magazine is popular among readers for its recipes.

BOOKS

Becoming Vegetarian
Vesanto Melina, R.D., Brenda Davis, R.D., and Victoria Harrison, R.D., Summertown, TN: Book Publishing Company, 1995.

Being Vegetarian
Suzanne Havala, M.S., R.D., F.A.D.A., for the American Dietetic Association, Minneapolis: Chronimed Publishing, 1996.

Eight Weeks to Optimum Health: A Proven Program for Taking Full Advantage of Your Body's Natural Healing Power
Andrew Weil, M.D., New York: Knopf, 1997

Good Foods, Bad Foods: What's Left to Eat?
Suzanne Havala, M.S., R.D., F.A.D.A., Minneapolis: Chronimed Publishing, 1998.

The Green Kitchen Handbook
Annie Berthold-Bond and Mothers & Others for a Livable Planet, New York: HarperCollins, 1997.

The Honest Herbal: A Sensible Guide to the Use of Herbs and Related Remedies, 3rd Edition
Tyler E. Varro, Ph.D., Hayworth Press, Binghamton, New York. *(See Aisle 6, page 107.)*

Safe Food: Eating Wisely in a Risky World
Michael Jacobson, Ph.D., Lisa Lefferts, and Anne Witte Garland, Los Angeles: Center for Science in the Public Interest, Living Planet Press, 1991.

The Safe Shopper's Bible: A Consumer's Guide to Nontoxic Household Products, Cosmetics, and Food
David Steinman and Samuel S. Epstein, M.D., New York: Macmillan, 1995.

Shopping for Health: A Nutritionist's Aisle-by-Aisle Guide to Smart, Low-Fat Choices at the Supermarket
Suzanne Havala, M.S., R.D., New York: HarperPerennial, 1996. (Available through the Book Publishing Company, Summertown, TN.)

Spontaneous Healing: How to Discover and Enhance Your Body's Natural Ability to Maintain and Heal Itself
Andrew Weil, M.D., New York: Ballantine Books, 1996.

The Use and Safety of Common Herbs and Herbal Teas, 2nd Edition
Winston Craig, Ph.D., Berrien Springs, MI: Golden Harvest Books, 1996. *(See Aisle 6, page 107 for ordering information.)*

The Vegetarian Food Guide and Nutrition Counter
Suzanne Havala, M.S., R.D., New York: The Berkley Publishing Group, 1997.

Vegetarian Journal's Guide to Natural Foods Restaurants in the U.S. and Canada
Vegetarian Resource Group, Garden City Park, NY: Avery Publishing Group, 1993.

The Vegetarian Way
Virginia Messina, M.P.H., R.D., and Mark Messina, Ph.D.,
New York: Crown Trade Paperbacks, 1996.

The Whole Food Bible
Chris Kilham, Rochester, Vermont: Inner Traditions Ltd.,
1996.

COOKBOOKS

The Complete Soy Cookbook
Paulette Mitchell, New York: Macmillan, 1998.

Conveniently Vegan: Turn Packaged Foods into Delicious Vegetarian Dishes
Debra Wasserman, Baltimore: Vegetarian Resource Group,
1997.

Fabulous Beans
Barb Bloomfield, Summertown, TN: The Book Publishing
Company, 1994.

Great Vegetarian Cooking Under Pressure: Two-Hour Taste in Ten Minutes
Lorna J. Sass, New York: William Morrow and Company,
1994.

Laurel's Kitchen Caring
Laurel Robertson, Berkeley, CA: Ten Speed Press, 1997.

Lean and Luscious and Meatless
Bobbie Hinman, Rocklin, CA: Prima Publishing, 1992.

The Meatless Gourmet: Favorite Recipes from Around the World
Bobbie Hinman, Rocklin, CA: Prima Publishing, 1995.

Mollie Katzen's Vegetable Heaven: Over 200 Recipes for Uncommon Soups, Tasty Bites, Side-by-Side Dishes, and Too Many Desserts
Mollie Katzen, New York: Hyperion, 1997.

The Moosewood Cookbook, New Revised Edition
Mollie Katzen, Berkeley, CA: Ten Speed Press, 1992.

The New Laurel's Kitchen
Laurel Robertson, Carol Flinders, and Brian Ruppenthal, Berkeley, CA: Ten Speed Press, 1986.

New Vegetarian Cuisine
Linda Rosensweig, Emmaus, PA: Rodale Press, 1994.

The Peaceful Palate, Revised Edition
Jennifer Raymond, Calistoga, CA: Heart and Soul Publications, 1418 Cedar Street, 94515-1610, 1992.

The Savory Way: High Spirited, Down-to-Earth Recipes from the Author of the Greens Cookbook
Deborah Madison, New York: Bantam Books, 1990.

Simply Vegan
Debra Wasserman and Reed Mangels, Baltimore: Vegetarian Resource Group, 1994.

Soy of Cooking: Easy-to-Make Vegetarian, Low-Fat, Fat-Free & Antioxidant-Rich Recipes
Marie Oser, Minneapolis: Chronimed Publishing, 1996.

Table for Two: Meat- and Dairy-Free Recipes for Two
Joanne Stepaniak, Summertown, TN: Book Publishing Company, 1996.

Tofu Cookery, Revised Edition
Louise Hagler, Summertown, TN: Book Publishing Company, 1991.

Vegetarian Cooking for Everyone
Deborah Madison, New York: Broadway Books, 1997.

The Vegetarian Hearth
Darra Goldstein, New York: HarperCollins, 1996.

Vegetarian Times Complete Cookbook
Editors of *Vegetarian Times*, New York: Macmillan, 1995.

NATURAL FOODS
TERMINOLOGY

Amaranth An ancient grain that was a staple food of the Aztecs in Central America. It grows as a broad-leafed plant that produces poppyseed-sized seeds. Amaranth is sold as a whole grain or flour and is used as an ingredient in commercial breakfast cereals and crackers sold in natural foods stores. It contains more protein than most cereal grains and is especially rich in the amino acids lysine and methionine.

Baba ganoujh (pronounced "bah bah gah NOOSH"): A dip or spread of Middle Eastern origin made primarily with blenderized eggplant, garlic, and tahini.

Certified Organic Foods that are certified organic meet state and voluntary standards for growing, handling, and processing. They are certified by independent, third-party, nonprofit agencies, and the standards can vary by state. Organic standards include practices that avoid the use of synthetic fertilizers and pesticides and use environmentally friendly agricultural methods. To be certified organic, foods must be grown on land that has been free of specified toxic substances for at least three years. A law has been passed authorizing the U.S. Department of

Agriculture to create uniform federal regulations, but these regulations have not been finalized as of this writing.

Couscous   Couscous is a traditional North African dish made from tiny round pieces of semolina, or durum wheat. Cooked couscous is mixed with tiny bits of fruit, with cooked vegetables, or with small pieces of meat. The grain is cooked by steaming it in a couscousière above a pot of sauce. It is thought that the word *couscous* comes from the sound of the steam rushing out of the couscousière.

Free-range   A term used to describe meat or eggs that come from animals that have been allowed to move freely around in their habitat as opposed to being confined in individual pens or cages. This is considered by many to be a more humane treatment of the animals than that which is practiced on factory farms. The humane treatment of animals that are raised for food is a value that is generally respected and promoted by the natural foods industry.

Herb   An herb is a plant or a component of a plant that is extracted or dried and used for its medicinal or aromatic qualities, or simply because it tastes good. Strictly speaking, though, the botanical term *herb* describes a nonwoody plant that produces seeds and is an annual, which means that at the end of the growing season it dies.

Hummus   A traditional Middle Eastern bean dip or spread made primarily with blenderized garbanzo beans (chickpeas), olive oil, garlic, lemon juice, and tahini.

Hydrogenated Fat   Fat that has been hardened by a process that changes the fat's chemical configuration. To create stick margarine, for instance, vegetable oil is hydrogenated so that it is firm enough to hold the shape of a stick. Oils are often partially hydrogenated to make

them firmer and to impart desired qualities to certain food
products. For instance, partially hydrogenated oil may be
blended into peanut butter to help the natural peanut oil
stay in suspension and not separate and rise to the surface
of the jar. Natural products do not contain hydrogenated
or partially hydrogenated fats.

Kamut (pronounced "kah MOOT"): A type of wheat that
has its roots in ancient Egypt.

Miso A traditional Japanese condiment that is used to flavor
foods and make miso soup. Miso has a rich, salty flavor. It
is made from soybeans and is aged and fermented according to a process that can take months or years.

Natural Foods There is no legal definition for the term
natural foods, but within the food industry it is generally
understood to describe foods that have been minimally
processed and are as close to their natural state as possible. They may have been altered by grinding, chopping,
drying, freezing, heating, fermenting, or separating, but
they have not been altered through a chemical process
(such as the hydrogenation of oils). They are generally
free of artificial flavorings and colorings, preservatives,
and any other additives that do not occur naturally in the
food.

Natural Products In addition to foods, natural products
stores carry nonfood items that conform to criteria that
are generally understood and complied with within the
industry. Nonfood products include personal care items
such as shampoos, soaps, cosmetics, lotions, and others.
These items are generally free of such ingredients as mineral oil, synthetic fragrances and dyes, petroleum, and
chemical preservatives. They are often free of animal by-
products and have not been tested on animals. Other nonfood natural products include household goods such as

cleaners and paper goods that tend to be environmentally friendly, as well as pet food, books, and magazines.

Organic   (see Certified Organic)

Phytochemicals   A wide range of substances found in plants that have biological activity in humans and help to protect our health. Examples include carotenoids such as beta-carotene and lycopene, isoflavones or phytoestrogens such as genistein, and possibly thousands of other substances.

Quinoa   (pronounced "KEEN wah"): A high-protein grain that was used by the Incas in Peru and is now popular around the world because of its nutritional value and pleasant flavor. Like amaranth, it is not a true cereal grain since it is the fruit of a plant and not a grass. Quinoa grains are tiny and flat and range in color from white or yellow to dark brown.

Rennetless Cheese   Rennet is an enzyme that comes from the lining of calves, pigs, lambs, or baby goats and is used to coagulate ripened dairy cheeses. Vegetarians avoid cheese made with rennet, and natural foods stores carry a wide selection of rennetless cheeses.

Soy Milk   A creamy milk made from whole soybeans that have been ground, cooked, and soaked. The milk is then pressed out of the beans. It has a mild "beanie" flavor that many people find quite appealing, though it also comes flavored vanilla, carob, and strawberry. Reduced-fat varieties are available, as are some that are fortified with extra vitamins and minerals. Packages are usually labeled "soy beverage" or "soy drink."

Spelt   A relative of wheat that has been popular in Europe for generations. It's being incorporated into grain products sold in American natural foods stores, and the flour is also available as whole spelt flour and white spelt flour.

Tabouli   A traditional Middle Eastern cold salad made primarily of bulgur wheat, minced vegetables, parsley, mint, olive oil, and lemon juice.

Tahini A paste or butter made of blenderized sesame seeds and used as an ingredient in traditional Middle Eastern foods such as baba ganoujh and hummus.

Teff One of the oldest cultivated grains. It originated in Ethiopia, where it is used to make the traditional, spongy, flat, round injera bread. Teff is a tiny grain that may be white, brown, or red in color.

Tempeh A traditional Indonesian soy food made from whole soybeans into a cultured bean cake. Sometimes mixed with a grain such as rice, the soybeans are fermented and pressed into the shape of a flat, rectangular block. Tempeh is highly nutritious and can be used in place of meat in such dishes as soups, stews, casseroles, and chili. It can be marinated and baked, grilled, or prepared in many other ways.

Tofu Soybean curd made by using a coagulant to curdle soy milk, separating the liquid from the solids, then pressing the solids into a block. A slightly different process is used to make silken tofu. Tofu is highly nutritious. It looks like a white block of spongy cheese, has little odor or flavor, but picks up the flavor of whatever it's cooked with.

Vegan Vegetarians who, in addition to not eating meat, fish, or poultry, do not eat or use other animal products and by-products, such as eggs, dairy products, honey, leather, fur, silk, wool, cosmetics, soaps, and other personal care items derived from animal products.

Vegetarian Persons who consume no meat, fish, or poultry or foods containing by-products of meat, fish, and poultry such as gelatin, meat flavorings or broths, and cheeses made with rennet. Lacto ovo vegetarians avoid meat, fish, and poultry but include dairy products and eggs in their diets. Lacto vegetarians avoid meat, fish, poultry, and eggs but include dairy products in their diets.

Whole Foods Foods as close to their natural state as possible and minimally processed as compared with other foods within a category. For instance, whole wheat flour is considered a whole food; white, refined flour is not.

INDEX

ABOUT THE AUTHOR

Suzanne Havala, M.S., R.D., F.A.D.A., is a licensed, registered dietitian and professional nutrition consultant. In addition to working with food companies, nonprofit groups, and other organizations, she writes books and articles and lectures to professionals and the general public. Among her special areas of interest are health and nutrition policy, food trends, and vegetarian diets.

She was the primary author of the American Dietetic Association's 1988 and 1993 position papers on vegetarian diets, and she is a founding member and former chairperson of the ADA's Vegetarian Nutrition Dietetic Practice Group. She is a nutrition adviser for the national, nonprofit Vegetarian Resource Group, and she serves on the editorial advisory board of *Vegetarian Times* magazine.

She is a past member of the ADA's State Media Representative/Ambassador Program. She is a regular contributor to *Vegetarian Journal* and *SELF* magazine, and she has written for *Vegetarian Times, Delicious!, Environmental Nutrition Newsletter, New Century Nutrition,* and the *Rochester Business Magazine.* She is frequently quoted in national magazines and newspapers, such as the *New York Times, Parade, Shape, Runner's World, New Woman, YM,*

Omni, Sassy, Harper's Bazaar, and many others, and has appeared on *Good Morning America,* the *Susan Powter Show,* and *Weekend Today in New York.*

She is the author of *The Complete Idiot's Guide to Being Vegetarian* (Alpha Books, 1999), *Good Foods, Bad Foods: What's Left to Eat?* (Chronimed Publishing, 1998), *The Vegetarian Food Guide and Nutrition Counter* (The Berkley Publishing Group, 1997), *Shopping for Health: A Nutritionist's Aisle-by-Aisle Guide to Smart, Low-fat Choices at the Supermarket* (HarperPerennial, 1996), and the American Dietetic Association's pocketbook, *Being Vegetarian* (Chronimed, 1996). She is also the author of *Simple, Lowfat & Vegetarian* (Vegetarian Resource Group, 1994) and cocreator of the *Shopping for Health* video series (Family Experiences Productions, Inc., 1997). She is a member of the National Association of Science Writers, the American Society of Journalists and Authors, the American Dietetic Association, and the American Public Health Association.

Suzanne is certified as a charter Fellow of the American Dietetic Association, a status granted to less than 1 percent of the 70,000 members of the ADA. She holds a bachelor of science degree with honor in dietetics from Michigan State University and a master of science degree in human nutrition from Winthrop University, Rock Hill, South Carolina. She is currently based in Chapel Hill, North Carolina, where she is a Public Health Leadership Doctoral Fellow in the department of health policy and administration in the School of Public Health at the University of North Carolina. She has been a vegetarian for twenty-four years.